NORTH CAROLINA
Off the Beaten Path

NORTH CAROLINA
Off the Beaten Path

by

Sara Pitzer

A Voyager Book

The Globe Pequot Press

Chester, Connecticut

Library of Congress Cataloging-in-Publication Data

Pitzer, Sara.
    North Carolina : off the beaten path / by Sara Pitzer. — 1st ed.
       p.   cm.
    "A Voyager book."
    ISBN 0-87106-478-2
    1. North Carolina—Description and travel—1981—Guide-books.
I. Title.
F252.3.P58 1990
917.5604'43—dc20   90-2891
                                        CIP

Cover Illustration by M.A. Dube
Interior Illustrations by Carole Drong
Cover: The Governor's Mansion in the Historic Oakwood district of Raleigh.

Manufactured in the United States of America
First Edition/First Printing

From now on, they're all for Croy.

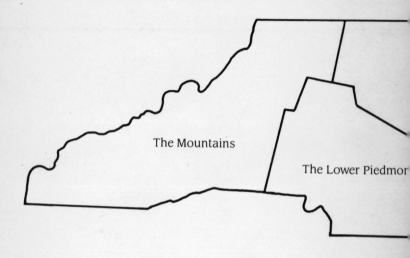

The Mountains

The Lower Piedmor

Contents

North Carolina

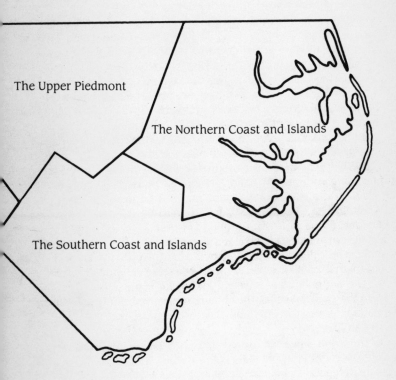

The Upper Piedmont

The Northern Coast and Islands

The Southern Coast and Islands

Introduction

I was lost—again—somewhere around Raleigh, but nowhere near the place I wanted to be. I'd already pulled into the entrance of a large industrial park, where an executive stopped on his way out to ask if he could help me. I'd already walked along the sidewalk in front of North Carolina State University, where a professor leaving campus gave me detailed instructions on getting out of the city in the direction I wanted to go. And I was pretty sure I was going to get it right, if I could just find the beltway. Seeing that the car in the next lane had both windows down as we waited for a light to turn, I called across to the driver, "Is this road going to take me to the beltway?"

"Where do you want to go?" he yelled back. I told him. "Follow me," he shouted, and when the light changed, took off in a cloud of exhaust. I followed him nearly 10 miles. At the proper entrance onto the beltway, he blinked his turn signal and also pointed emphatically with his left hand, just in case I missed the signal. I turned. He was already gone, leaving me with a grin and a wave.

And that's how people in North Carolina are.

For me, living in North Carolina is no accident of birth nor whim of corporate transfer; it's a studied choice. When my husband and I decided that we should both work free lance, it meant that we could live pretty much wherever we wanted to. We spent the better part of a year looking for a place where the topography was appealing, the climate was sunny and temperate, the economy was thriving, and the people were nice. We found North Carolina.

In the years since we moved here in 1983, life has been one joyful discovery about the state after another. Indeed, sometimes it seems too good to believe. Many mornings I wake up thinking: Today's the day I'm going to be disappointed. But I never am.

I know you'll enjoy my discoveries too.

Take the barbecue, for instance. Two authors writing an article on southern barbecue for *Cook's* magazine traveled through several states looking for the best barbecue restaurants, but they were not able to get to North Carolina. They apologized in their article, because, they said, in comparison, nothing else is barbecue at all. (North Carolina barbecue is always pork cooked over a wood fire, never prepared in a sauce, and usually served with slaw and hush puppies.)

Then there's the pottery. This state has scores and scores of potters, working in the historic old production styles and in contemporary studio modes, producing such a variety of work that a collection could easily crowd everything else from a room.

As for topography, North Carolina has some of the oldest mountains in the world, the largest natural sand dune on the East Coast, and some of the most unspoiled beaches and islands in the country. The rich soil of the Piedmont and foothills grows apples, vegetables, Christmas trees, cotton, and tobacco, a problematic crop with much historic significance.

Also historically important, North Carolina, one of the thirteen original colonies, played important roles in the revolutionary war, the Civil War, and World Wars I and II. The area is rich in Indian history; blacks have made many early significant advances here; and the Moravians created a historic settlement at Old Salem. The Wright brothers first accomplished powered flight in North Carolina, on a site that is popular today with hang gliders more interested in playing than in setting records.

Each of the three major geographic areas of the state—the coastal plain, the Piedmont, and the mountains—differs radically from the others. It's almost like traveling through three smaller states. The nature of each region influenced the kinds of commerce that flourished historically and continue to flourish, and also left a mark on the people. As you travel, you'll hear fascinating changes in the music of the accents of people native to each region.

The coastal plain accounts for almost two-fifths of the state's area. The North Carolina coast has been considered dangerous since the first settlers tried to cope with its ever-changing beaches, currents, and waterways. There was no guarantee that just because you had safely sailed into a particular port once you would find it safe, or even open, the next time you tried. That's at least one reason why English colonization shifted up toward the Chesapeake and why North Carolina was settled more sparsely and slowly than some other colonies. Even today you find areas that are remarkably sparsely settled compared to most states' coastal regions. For vacationers, the main activities and sightseeing are related to the same activities that have supported the area economically—fishing, boats, and beaches.

Introduction

In the Piedmont, which makes up about another two-fifths of the state, you find mostly rolling hills and red clay. Although the clay is harder to work than the sandy soil of the coast, it seems to have held better its fertility against some pretty bad early farming habits. (Wherever they are grown, cotton and tobacco are notorious for wearing out the soil.) Since the Piedmont doesn't have many large stretches of flat land, it didn't invite the huge plantations that had to be worked with many slaves. Smaller family farms were often worked by the people who owned them, perhaps with some hired help. The historians Hugh Talmage Lefler and Albert Ray Newsome point out in their classic *The History of a State: North Carolina* that the narrow, swift streams of the Piedmont, which weren't worth much for transportation, were great for generating power. And that, along with the presence of hardwoods and other resources, accounts for the great number of manufacturing activities that flourish in the Piedmont. Here you find lots of attractions related to manufacturing—tobacco museums, furniture showrooms, and more outlet stores than you can count. Probably because of the past concentration of moneyed manufacturers and merchants, you'll also find rich lodes of cultural attractions and arts here.

The mountains make up the smallest part of the state, but they compensate in interest and beauty for what they lack in area. Some of the highest mountains in the Appalachians are here. As anyone who drives in the mountains knows, transportation is difficult. In earlier times it was nearly impossible, hence the development of small pockets of civilization separated by stretches of wilderness, creating those tough, independent, resourceful, self-sufficient folks—mountain people. This kind of early self-sufficiency and distance from major metropolitan areas made the growth of all kinds of crafts almost inevitable. The mountains are still the richest source of handcrafts in the state.

Although tourism and technology have homogenized somewhat the state's regional populations, you can still find lots of those tall, thin, rangy people. It remains a pretty good joke in the Piedmont for a young woman marrying outside the area to claim she's found herself a mountain man.

Of course, today the immigration of Yankees from "up north" and considerable growth mean that every region has its share of developers, builders, and real estate people. These activities, however, tend to be clustered mostly around the major cities and a few popular mountain and beach resort areas. There are still lots of places off the beaten path to go for fun.

As a place to play, the state offers hiking and white-water rafting, water-skiing and snow skiing, freshwater and saltwater fishing and boating, athletics, auto racing, horseback riding, and golf on some of the most famous courses in the country.

Face it, you're not going to be able to do it all or see it all in one trip, or even in ten trips. Don't try to squeeze too much into a single trip, or you'll end up driving a lot and not doing much else. But the driving you do shouldn't be unpleasant if you avoid the interstates around major cities at rush hour and accept the fact that the two-lane roads tend to be well maintained but slow, since there are few good places for passing slow drivers and tractors. To understand the roads and decide when to travel on a major highway and when to get onto secondary roads, you'll definitely need a state map. The best one is the North Carolina transportation map, issued by the North Carolina Department of Transportation and the Division of Travel and Tourism (919-733-4171). You may pick one up free at a welcome center or receive it by writing North Carolina Division of Travel and Tourism, 430 North Salisbury Street, Raleigh, 27611.

If you or those traveling with you are in any way physically challenged, you should also request a copy of the book *Access, North Carolina.* This is a remarkably good book published by the North Carolina Department of Human Resources, the Division of Vocational Rehabilitation Services, and the Division of Travel and Tourism. It briefly describes historic sites, state and national parks and forests, and general interest attractions, focusing on their accessibility of parking, entrance, interior rooms, exterior areas, and rest rooms. The book is free.

A state with so many resources inevitably becomes the subject of many books. Depending on your interests, you may find several of them interesting to use along with this guide. The University of North Carolina Press publishes *Turners and Burners: The Folk Potters of North Carolina,* by Charles G. Zug III, the most complete explication of the subject available. The press also publishes many books about North Carolina history. For further information, write University of North Carolina Press, P.O. Box 2288, Chapel Hill, 27514.

If you are a devotee of back roads, you may enjoy Earl Thollander's *Back Roads of the Carolinas,* devoted entirely to "nonhighway" drives along roads that often aren't on regular maps. Thollander designed the book, lettered the text in calligraphy, and drew the maps and wash illustrations himself. Often Thollander suggests a dirt road or other obscure route from one historic point to another, which you could use as a much, much slower alternative to the routes I suggest. It is published by Clarkson N. Potter, Inc., One Park Avenue, New York, NY 10016. Finally, the North Carolina publisher John F. Blair (1406 Plaza Drive, Winston-Salem, 27103-1485) offers several books about the history and ecology of the North Carolina coast, plus an appealing book of photographs and native comment, *Ocracoke Portrait*, by Ann Ehringhaus, whose bed and breakfast inn on Ocracoke appears in this guidebook. It's especially fun to read such books ahead of time and then carry them with you to consult, because the material comes alive as you see the subject matter firsthand.

With or without the books, though, North Carolina comes alive when you travel here because of its people. Significant history, appealing countryside, even good food can be part of any well-planned trip. Adding helpful, friendly, almost uniformly cheerful people changes the mix from plain cake to an angel food celebration. In the years I've been traveling almost continuously about the state, I've not had a single unpleasant experience with a North Carolinian. Unless you carry a chip the size of one of Mount Mitchell's ancient trees on your shoulder, you won't either. And if you're in that bad a mood, don't come. If you can't have fun in North Carolina, you can't enjoy yourself anywhere. Might as well stay home.

The prices and rates listed in this guidebook were confirmed at press time. We recommend, however, that you call establishments before traveling to obtain current information.

Off the Beaten Path in The Southern Coast and Islands

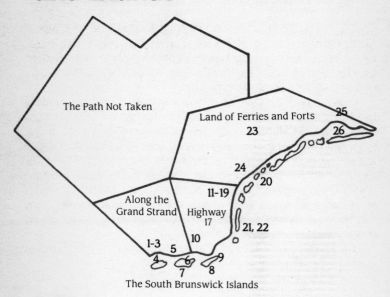

The Path Not Taken

Land of Ferries and Forts

25

23

26

24

20

11–19

Along the Grand Strand

Highway

17

21, 22

1-3

5

10

4

6

9

7

8

The South Brunswick Islands

1. Calabash
2. Captain Jim's Marina
3. Ella's Restaurant
4. Sunset Beach
5. Italian Fisherman
6. Ocean Isle
7. Scheffield's Marina
8. Holden Beach
9. North Carolina Oyster Festival
10. Sim's Country Bar-B-Que, Inc. II
11. Historic Wilmington District
12. St. John's Museum of Art
13. The Inn on Orange
14. Chandler's Wharf
15. The Riverboat Landing Restaurant
16. Elizah's Oyster Bar
17. Cotton Exchange
18. USS *North Carolina* Battleship Memorial
19. *Henrietta II*
20. Wrightsville Beach
21. Fort Fisher National Historic Site
22. North Carolina Aquarium
23. Duplin Wine Cellars
24. Poplar Grove Plantation
25. Cedar Point
26. Meko's Restaurant

The Southern Coast and Islands

Along the Grand Strand

Like most of this country's coastal areas, the beaches of North Carolina attract plenty of tourists, but some have so far managed to avoid the near honky-tonk atmosphere of the better-known places such as Myrtle Beach, just below the North Carolina—South Carolina border.

Close enough to that border to confuse anyone who misses the North Carolina welcome center on Highway 17, the little community of **Calabash** comes as a surprise to all but the people who visit beaches in the area regularly. The sign proclaiming Calabash the seafood capital of the world seems bigger than the town, which covers only a couple of miles and has only a couple hundred permanent residents. But you'll find more than thirty restaurants, all specializing in seafood. Mostly they're owned and run by local fishing families, are invariably casual, and feature fresh "Calabash-style" deep-fried seafood.

Calabash-style means the seafood has a light, almost tempura, batter coating. Of course it's served with hush puppies; it's easier to separate income and tax than it is to get seafood in Calabash without hush puppies. Oyster roasts are as popular as the fried seafood. When you order an oyster roast, you're brought a huge kettle full of oysters steamed just until they open, a shucking knife to prod the oysters out of their shells, a dish of melted butter, a roll of paper towels, and a wastebasket to catch the oyster shells as you empty them.

Any number of restaurants claim to be the original Calabash restaurant and to have the authentic recipe for Calabash-style seafood. One of the most established and best is Captain Nance's Seafood Restaurant, on the Calabash River (which is full of shrimp, crabs, and flounder). The restaurant is open from 11:00 A.M. to 9:00 P.M. seven days a week, year-round (919-579-2574).

Nearby, also on the Calabash River, **Captain Jim's Marina** charters boats at reasonable rates for full- and half-day fishing. If you enjoy the sport but hate the mess that follows, you'll appreciate the free fish-cleaning service. And if you find the whole fishing thing just too gory for words, you're a likely customer for an evening riding cruise. The marina is open every day from 8:00 A.M. to 12:30 P.M. and 1:00 to 5:30 P.M. If you're seriously interested in boating, you should call ahead (919-579-3660), as weather, special charters, and slow seasons can affect the regular schedule.

A smaller restaurant with a strong family feel that you might miss just driving through the area is **Ella's Restaurant,** a pleasant place for seafood and a beer or soft drink. Ella's presumably has fed a full share of rainy-day customers, because the following legend is displayed near the front: Coil up your ropes and anchor here/ till better weather doth appear. To get to Ella's, turn onto Highway 179, at the only red light in Calabash, heading toward the water. You can seek food or shelter from 11:00 A.M. to 10:00 P.M., seven days a week, year-round.

In the summer Calabash is very busy, attracting tourists from Myrtle Beach as well as from the beaches to the north. The marina and the better restaurants, however, operate year-round, and in slower seasons a stop in Calabash is low-key and can be fun.

The South Brunswick Islands

Driving north on Highway 17 just over 10 miles takes you to the beginning of the South Brunswick Islands. Sunset Beach, Ocean Isle, and Holden Beach differ from one another as much as the siblings in most families. Part of the chain of barrier islands off the coast that stretches both north and south, the South Brunswick Islands have no boardwalks and relatively little commercial development except for beach houses and a few small grocery stores.

In the fall of 1989, Hurricane Hugo accentuated an interesting phenomenon along Holden Beach, Ocean Isle, and Sunset Beach. The hurricane didn't do any more damage than any good storm does, breaking up some docks, flooding some first-floor rooms in cabins, and lifting off a piece of roof here and there. But it moved the beaches, literally, hastening an erosion process that was already obvious, moving sand and dunes from the east and depositing them farther west. This means that beachfront at Holden Beach grows noticeably more narrow with each storm, as does the east end of Ocean Isle's beachfront, leading to black-humor jokes suggesting that the way to get an oceanfront property here is to buy third row and wait. Meanwhile the beaches on the west end of Ocean Isle and those on Sunset Beach are visibly growing more and more broad. It takes regular dredging to keep the waterway between Ocean Isle and Sunset Beach open because the currents continue to dump sand there. Beaches have broadened so much at Sunset Beach that when you stand at water's edge, you can't see the first-row cottages behind the dunes. It sounds like good, forward-thinking planning; actually, it's nature.

This shifting creates some problems for developers and homeowners but does not in any way spoil the pleasure of visiting any of the islands. Indeed, if you're interested in the ecology of coastlines, try to find a copy of *The Beaches are Moving*, by Wallace Kaufman and Orrin H. Pilkey, Jr., published by Duke University Press in 1979. The book describes, explains, and predicts such activity, though it focuses on beaches along both the east and west coasts and doesn't talk specifically about the South Brunswick Islands. Browsing through the book, which is rich in historical data and information about how tides, storms, and so on work, while you stay in the South Brunswick Islands is like having your very own little nature model to study as you read. It's great fun and genuinely instructive.

Access to **Sunset Beach** still depends on a one-lane swing bridge across the Intracoastal Waterway. A swing bridge differs from a drawbridge in that the movable part of the bridge swings to the side rather than lifting up to allow tall ships to pass under. It's unique in these times. It's also threatened. Developers have plans to replace it with a higher, modern bridge that would accommodate more traffic faster. At the moment, people who like the sleepy, undeveloped atmosphere of Sunset Beach are fighting to stop the new bridge. They'll probably lose. But, at least for the immediate future, this is a place with only a few paved roads and sidewalks, no high-rise condos, and no pink giraffes or water slides or beachfront grills. What the island does have is glorious, wide, flat beaches and clean white sand. From most of the beach area, you can't see any buildings at all. The beach homes, most of which are available for rent, sit hidden behind the dunes. The best way to enjoy Sunset Beach is to rent one of these houses. They are handled by three realty rental agents. The newest of these, which may therefore be trying harder, is the Odom Company, which does everything from letting you go directly to your rental home instead of stopping to check in at the office to lending you crab traps and charcoal grills. The office (919–579–3515 or 919–579–6201) is open seven days a week, year-round, from 9:00 A.M. to 5:00 P.M. During the summer season cottage rentals are usually by the week, Saturday to Saturday. Other times are more flexible.

Also, at the Sunset Beach Motel (919–579–7093), near where the bridge comes onto the island, you can rent rooms.

Whether you stay awhile or just pass through, a nice place to stop for dinner is the **Italian Fisherman,** on the mainland right next to the bridge that crosses the waterway to the island. The restaurant is one of the thoroughly established operations in the area that attracts customers year-round. In addition to seafood prepared with Italian seasonings, you can order several fine veal dishes, a variety of pasta dishes, and wonderful fried calamari. This is the kind of place where the same people work year after year and remember those visitors who return. Although there is a complete bar, and drinks are served in the dining rooms as well, the atmosphere is holiday casual, and entire families, including babies in high chairs, can eat comfortably here. The guests tend to be as friendly as the staff, often striking up conversations from one table to another. One summer evening an eighteen-month-old in a high chair was doing a standard smear job on her face, head, and hair with spaghetti. A diner at the next table snapped a picture of the scene and later sent it to the child's parents. The Italian Fisherman (919–579–2929) is open seven days a week during the summer season, from 5:00 to 9:00 P.M. In the off-season the restaurant is open only Wednesday through Sunday. In November the days are Thursday through Sunday. They are usually busy, so reservations are a very good idea.

The next island north is **Ocean Isle.** To get there, drive north on Highway 17 about 5 miles and turn right onto Route 179 South, which takes you directly to the Odell Williamson Bridge, across the Intracoastal Waterway. The fact that the island was originally settled in 1954 by Odell and his family, who rowed across the waterway after Hurricane Hazel to get to the island, tells you something about the island. The Williamson family still runs a lively rental, sales, and building business on the island. Although there is a water slide, you'll find little other commercial development here. This island is more settled, with sidewalks, all-paved roads, some cluster homes and condos on the west end,

5

and more traditional beach homes on the east end. Also on the east end, a series of paved and natural canals, where the homes have docks, can accommodate boats or just provide pleasant off-ocean outdoor lounging space. A few hundred permanent residents live on the island. Their homes are mingled among those used strictly for vacation and rental. It's a nice mix, and especially if you do not stay in beachfront properties, you can learn a lot about the island from these people and form friendships that continue past your visit. Williamson Realty, one of several that handle island homes, is pleasant to deal with if you want to rent a cottage or condo. Their Saturday-to-Saturday rental schedule during the season, with more flexibility at other times, operates much the same as on Sunset Beach. The office (919-579-2373 or 579-2858) is open from 9:00 A.M. to 5:00 P.M., Monday through Saturday, and Sunday from noon to 4:00 P.M. (closed on Sundays during December, January, and February).

The Island Motel (919-579-3599) rents rooms by the night, but you lose a lot of the community feeling staying either in a motel or beachfront accommodation.

Whatever you do while you're at Ocean Isle, spend some time at **Scheffield's Marina.** It has a boat dock in back, automobile gas pumps in front, groceries, fishing supplies, and beer inside, and the nicest people imaginable everywhere. You can buy just-caught shrimp and fish, newly dug clams, all the fixin's to go with them, and in the process, trade recipes with the proprietors for preparing whatever you bought. Scheffield's (919-579-2574) is open from 7:30 A.M. to 9:00 P.M. (10:00 P.M. on weekends) seven days a week, year-round.

Standing on the west end of Ocean Isle, you can see Sunset Beach. It looks close enough to wade over, which old-timers remember doing before erosion and currents changed the shape of the islands. Standing on the east end of Ocean Isle, you see **Holden Beach,** also seeming almost close enough to wade across. Without a boat, though, getting to Holden Beach takes a drive of about fifteen minutes. Richard Mubel, the news editor for the *State Port Pilot,* once wrote for the *Brunswick Magazine* that Holden is a place where "old meets new, where tradition bisects progress and where history intersects the path of the future." He's talking about the contrasts between the backside of the island, along the Atlantic Intracoastal Waterway and the Lockwood Folly River Inlet, and the oceanfront. Shrimpers and fishermen descended from families who settled the area still work along the waterway and inlet, as well as in the open sea, but the oceanfront is strictly a vacationland of white beaches and summer cottages. You'll find more shopping in this area, but compared to major coastal resort areas, it's still quiet and appeals to people who like a little more activity than can be found at Sunset or Ocean Isle without getting into plastic, chrome, and glass. Half a dozen rental agents renting cottages and condos, a campground, and a motel serve the area. Alan Holden Realty has the most properties and friendly people to answer the phone. They're open from 9:00 A.M. to 5:00 P.M. seven days a week, year-round. The Gray Gull Motel (919-842-6775), an older but clean establishment, rents individual rooms.

If you enjoy local festivals and if you lo-o-o-o-ve seafood, try to schedule your Brunswick Island trip for the third weekend in October, for the annual **North Carolina Oyster Festival**. This festival began as a small oyster roast in the late 1970s. Every year the party got a little better and in three years got itself proclaimed the official oyster festival of North Carolina. It takes a couple hundred community volunteers to run the event, which now includes a beach run, a bullshooting (tall-tale-telling) contest, and the North Carolina Oyster Shucking Championship. This contest is no small potatoes. It has produced not only a national Oyster Shucking Champion, but also the top female oyster shucker in the world. With all that shucking going on, it stands to figure somebody's got to be doing some eating. That's where you come in. Steamed oysters, fried oysters, oysters on the half shell, boiled shrimp, fried flounder, and of course the ubiquitous hush puppies are available in abundance. Food is served from noon to 7:00 P.M. on Saturday and, on a more limited scale, from 1:00 to 5:00 P.M. on Sunday. In addition to the food and contests, the festival features two days of live music that includes beach music (shag), top forty, country and western, and gospel. Also artists and craftspeople display their wares for sale. For fuller details and firm dates in any year, call the South Brunswick Islands Chamber of Commerce (919-754-6644).

Highway 17

The Brunswick Isles are served by businesses in the town of Shalotte, a few miles inland on Highway 17. This is the place to stop when you need to do laundry or pick up a bicycle pump from the hardware store or get a prescription filled in a good-sized pharmacy. It's also where you'll find **Sims Country Bar-B-Que, Inc. II,** Michael Sims, manager. Here you can order good pork barbecue. No North Carolina travel writer who wants to live would dare call any one barbecue better than the others. Sims also serves tasty beef and chicken barbecue. The atmosphere is absolutely picnic table, oilcloth, mason jar, down-home local. Entertainment in the evenings includes bluegrass music and square dancing. Consistent with the religious beliefs of many in the area, the festivities proceed without beer, wine, or liquor. They're serious about this; Sims doesn't sell it, and you may not bring it in. If you spend time here, order the pork barbecue plate, get someone else to try the chicken and snitch a piece, drink iced tea, and enjoy the wholesomeness of it all. The easiest way to find Sims is to backtrack a couple of miles after you're finished shopping in the Shalotte business area, going south on Highway 17 to where it intersects with Highway 904 at Grissettown. Turn right on Highway 904, toward Longwood and Tabor City. Almost immediately you will come to a right-hand turn that leads you to Sims Country Bar-B-Que. Signs help you. The restaurant (919-287-3225) is open from 5:00 to 9:00 P.M. on Friday and Saturday April to June; Thursday, Friday, and Saturday June to September; and Friday and Saturday from September to Thanksgiving.

From Shalotte, driving north on Highway 17 for a little less than an hour brings you to Wilmington. People who live here call Wilmington the best-kept secret in North Carolina. They're of two minds as to whether that's good or bad. The thriving, historic community has a full share of entrepreneurial types who've done much to revitalize waterfront areas and old downtown buildings. They welcome tourists and new business. Some of the old-timers would rather the community's cultural and historical attractions not become too well known, lest all the new traffic spoil the ambience.

In 1989, Wilmington, which was settled before the revolutionary war and during the Civil War was the last Atlantic port open to blockade runners, celebrated its 250th anniversary. Historic restoration and preservation in the official **Historic Wilmington District** have produced an appealing neighborhood from which you can take the Historic Wilmington House Tour. This guided walking tour gives you a chance to see five of the most outstanding buildings in the city and see the interiors of two of these, which have been beautifully restored: the 1770 Burgin-Wright House and the 1852 Zebulon Latimer House. The tour, which takes ninety minutes, includes the Orton, Airlie, and Greenfield gardens of azaleas and cypress trees. Tours are offered at 10:00 A.M., 11:00 A.M., noon, 1:00 P.M., 2:00 P.M., and 3:00 P.M., Tuesday through Saturday. Tickets are modestly priced. The box office is at 118 Princess Street (919-763-9328 or 763-3398).

Another pleasant way to see the historic area is to take a sight-seeing tour by horse-drawn carriage, with a driver who narrates as you pass the historic sites. Tours begin at the corner of Water and Market streets. They run from 11:00 A.M. to 10:00 P.M., Tuesday through Sunday, from April through October. During November, December, and March, from 7:00 to 10:00 P.M., Friday, Saturday and Sunday. Other times may be arranged by appointment (919-251-8889). Moderate rates.

One attraction that definitely deserves more attention is **St. John's Museum of Art,** at 114 Orange Street (919-763-0281). The museum, which is tastefully light and airy, comprises three historic buildings: a Masonic Lodge (1804), the Cowan House Studio (c. 1830), and what was St. Nicholas Greek Orthodox Church (1943). A sculpture garden ties the complex together. The permanent collection features 200 years of North Carolina art. The most important gift the museum has received is the original color prints of Mary Cassatt, the nineteenth-century American artist who worked with the Impressionists in France. The museum also has a dozen temporary exhibitions that change annually. Open Tuesday through Saturday, 10:00 A.M. to 5:00 P.M., and Sunday, noon to 4:00 P.M. Admission free.

Also on Orange Street is a nice place to spend the night, **The Inn on Orange,** near the center of the historic district (919-251-0863). Catherine Ackiss epitomizes old-style southern hospitality, which is just what she intends to do. It all started a few years ago when she decided to leave her job in department store promotion in Raleigh. She and her husband were driving through Wilmington, and she said, "Walter, I want to be a hostess!" To get the feel of this story you've got to read that line something like, "WALLta, ah wont toe be a HOEstess!" And you must hear the exclamation point. Catherine and Walter found the recently renovated old home at 410 Orange Street just waiting for her to set up her inn. Many of the furnishings, including a piano Catherine refinished herself, belonged to her family. For all the elegance and antiques, the place feels comfortably homey and has become especially popular with traveling business people and newlyweds looking for something more personal than the glass and chrome of a hotel. One young woman executive came into the inn saying, "All the time I was driving here I kept thinking, 'I can't wait to get there and tell Catherine about this new guy I went out with.'" Catherine is one of those innkeepers who says, and means, that when you walk through the door you become a member of her family.

Early in the morning, Catherine sets up a coffee and tea service in the hallway outside your bedroom door, followed by a full homemade breakfast in the dining room later. Another enticement is that the inn has a swimming pool in the backyard. Rates are moderate.

From the inn, you can walk to **Chandler's Wharf,** on the Cape Fear River, a complex of restored historical warehouses and buildings with cobblestone streets, picket fences, and pretty streams. Instead of maritime businesses, the buildings now hold specialty shops and restaurants. **The Riverboat Landing Restaurant** (919-763-7227) is operated by an Italian family but offers many more seafood specialties than pasta dishes. It's a casual place where you're at ease either in dressy or tourist clothes, and even fussy kids do OK here because while you're enjoying fresh grouper or cioppino, others can have spaghetti or lasagna. And even though the proprietors are playing down their Italian offerings to promote their seafood (They say, "Remember, Italians are fishermen too") they make a wicked cannoli that no one should miss. Beer, wine, and mixed drinks are available in the lounge and dining room. In good weather, some of the nicest dining areas are those on outdoor and glass-enclosed balconies overlooking the river. Prices are moderate. Open for lunch 11:30 A.M. to 5:00 P.M., and dinner 5:00 P.M. to 1:00 A.M. Monday through Thursday. Open until 2:00 A.M. Saturday. Open 5:00 P.M. to 1:00 A.M. Sunday.

Also in Chandler's Wharf, **Elizah's Oyster Bar,** on the waterfront, is open from 11:30 A.M. to midnight, Tuesday through Saturday. The place is known for its hot crab dip and good house wines.

Another complex of eight restored old buildings, the **Cotton Exchange** (919-343-9896), beginning on Front Street between Walnut and Grace, features almost thirty shops and restaurants, including Paddy's Hollow, a Victorian pub, and East Bank Trading Company, a shop of American handcrafts. Most of the shops are open from 10:00 A.M. to 5:00 P.M., Monday through Saturday, and from 1:00 to 5:00 P.M., Sunday. The restaurants are open evenings as well.

From all these points along the river, you can see the **USS North Carolina Battleship Memorial,** commissioned in 1941 and considered the world's greatest battleship at the time. The ship has been docked as a memorial since 1961. The self-guided tour, which takes about two hours, leads you through the crew's quarters, galley, sick bay, engine room, and pilothouse. What you see is fascinating in its technical detail. If you're the kind of person who embarrasses genteel guides in historic homes by asking what they used for toilet paper, this tour is definitely for you. A short orientation film starts you off.

The USS *North Carolina* Battleship

A more glitzy approach to the same ship is the outdoor sound and light show, "The Immortal Showboat," offered every night at 9:00 P.M. from the first Friday in June through Labor Day. The audience sits in a 1,000-seat grandstand across from the ship's port bow, while voices, lights, music, and special-effect ordnance fire dramatize the ship's history for seventy minutes. The ship looms out of the water where Highways 17, 74, 76, and 421 intersect, 3 miles outside Wilmington. In addition to a good-sized parking lot, you'll find a center for visitors with a gift shop, snack bar, and picnic shelter. The ship (919-762-1829) is open every day of the year from 8:00 A.M. to sunset. Write USS *North Carolina* Battleship Memorial, P.O. Box 417, Wilmington, 28402.

During the summer an alternative to parking at the battleship site is to take the Riverboat Taxi over from Chandler's Wharf. Originally it was a World War II U.S. Navy launch. It leaves every half hour for the battleship from 10:00 A.M. to 5:00 P.M. daily. Modest rates.

You can't get seasick on the battleship unless you have a wildly vivid imagination, and the launch ride is too short to do much damage. If you'd like to test your sea legs a bit more realistically, you could try a riverboat cruise on the ***Henrietta II,*** which docks at the foot of Market Street on the Cape Fear River. These cruises are party affairs, ranging from Sunday sightseeing cruises to evening Dogwood cruises in spring, a sweetheart cruise on Valentine's Day, and weekend dinner cruises. It's all planned and public, but if you're in the mood for it, the gaiety can be a lot of fun. The original *Henrietta* was the first steam paddleboat built in North Carolina, and it ran the river between Wilmington and Fayetteville for forty years. James Seawell (no joke), the builder, named it for his daughter. The *Henrietta II* is a nearly new paddleboat and includes a dance floor and an air-conditioned dining room, in addition to the outdoor deck space you'd expect. If she can see this modern version, poor *Henrietta* is probably wishing herself back to the future.

Land of Ferries and Forts

Just a few miles away from the historic port of Wilmington you come to a series of beaches: Wrightsville, Carolina, Wilmington, and Kure. The entire area has more historic sites and interesting spots to visit than can be included in a book covering the entire state. For folks seeking out-of-the-way places, the beaches don't offer the same secluded charm as the Brunswick Islands, but they can be fun, with enough amusement and entertainment to please the kids without doing in Mother and Dad, especially if you avoid the peak summer season. And a number of historical and marine attractions are especially important and interesting. **Wrightsville Beach** is 12 miles east of Wilmington. It operates as a year-round island resort and has plenty of motels and some nice, casual, moderately priced seafood restaurants.

Driving south from Wilmington on Highway 421 for a little less than 20 miles takes you to the beaches on Pleasure Island. All this area is highly commercial and built up, but if you stick it out to Kure Beach, you'll find two attractions worth taking time to see if you're interested in the naval aspects of Civil War history and in marine life.

Three miles south of Kure Beach, on Highway 421, is **Fort Fisher National Historic Site.** The fort stood up under heavy naval attack during the Civil War, and some of the 25-foot earthwork fortifications that protected the Cape Fear River and the port of Wilmington from Union forces remain. Reading about such parapets is one thing; looking at them and musing on how they must have been built before the days of bulldozers is a more vivid experience, intensified by such touches as a reconstruction of the gun placement and a history trail. There's also a museum that displays Civil War artifacts and offers a slide show on the history of the fort. If you travel with a picnic cooler, you'll enjoy the picnic area on the site. Admission free (919–458-5538). Open April through October, 9:00 A.M. to 5:00 P.M. Monday through Saturday, 1:00 to 5:00 P.M. Sunday; November through March, 9:00 A.M. to 5:00 P.M. Tuesday through Saturday, 1:00 to 4:00 P.M. Sunday, and closed Monday.

Across from Fort Fisher Historic Site, the **North Carolina Aquarium** features a twenty-thousand-gallon shark aquarium, a whale exhibit, and a touch tank where children (and adults too, for that matter) can actually handle some kinds of marine life. There are also koi (carp) pools and river otters. The aquarium maintains a full schedule of special events and educational programs. It might be worth calling ahead for a schedule (919–458-8257). Admission is free. Open 9:00 A.M to 5:00 P.M., Monday through Saturday, and 1:00 to 5:00 P.M., Sunday. Closed Thanksgiving, Christmas, and New Year's Day.

When you get this far south on the island, you will have two choices. You can take the Fort Fisher Ferry to Southport, which brings you close to the Brunswick Islands, whence you began driving, or you can backtrack up the island and take the bridge across to Wilmington, also whence you began driving. At first glance, the obvious way to avoid those whences and the dilemma of decision would be to begin by taking the ferry from Southport to Fort Fisher, then drive north on the island and finally cross over to the delights of Wilmington. You may indeed decide to do it that way, especially if you're not traveling during the peak summer months. But you need to know that the ferry only leaves Southport seven times a day; crossing takes an hour; it accommodates only twenty automobiles at a time; and the time schedule may change. Trying to learn and meet a schedule only to end up waiting in a line that has cut off several cars ahead of you because the ferry is already full is not the stuff relaxing vacations are made of. For more current information when you decide, phone (919) 458-3329. Some information is also available from the Cape Fear Coast Convention and Visitors Bureau (800-222-4757 in the eastern U.S., 800-922-7117 in NC, or 919-341-4030).

Should you decide to backtrack to Wilmington, you can give the kids a pleasant break by stopping at the Tote-em-in Zoo, about 10 miles south of Wilmington on Highway 421. The zoo, which has been in business more than thirty-five years, features more than a hundred different animals, a museum of exotic mounted speci- mens, and another museum of varied artifacts from around the world, including arrowheads and World War II items. Modest rates. Open from spring thaw until the first hard freeze, roughly March through November, 8:30 A.M. to 4:30 P.M. weekdays and until 6:30 P.M. weekends. In the off-season, especially after school starts, the hours may be shorter (919-791-0472).

If you're interested in North Carolina wineries, you may want to schedule a side trip while you're in the Wilmington area to **Duplin Wine Cellars,** about an hour's drive from the coast. The winery is in Rose High, on Highway 117, about halfway between Wilmington and Goldsboro. The winery conducts tours and tastings and, of course, sells the wines. Tours are preceded by an audiovisual presentation on the history of southern winemaking. Duplin Wine Cellars (919-289-3888) is especially well known for its Magnolia, a soft dry table wine, and its scuppernong dessert wine. The word *scuppernong* is an Indian word meaning "sweet tree."

Scuppernong is the oldest grape in America, and the Duplin Cellars is the only winery in America that makes 100 percent scuppernong wine. Open Monday through Saturday, 9:00 A.M. to 5:00 P.M. Closed New Year's Day, July 4, Labor Day, Thanksgiving Day, and Christmas Day. Write for a free newsletter: P.O. Box 756, Rose Hill 28458.

From Wilmington, the best way to head north is to drive on Highway 17 for a while. Stretches of it are annoyingly full of strip-city areas where traffic is heavy and slow. Taking some of the little side roads seems like a good idea, and you can if you wish without fear of getting lost, because most of them eventually loop back to Highway 17 anyway. But the loops are disappointing. You won't find much but scrubland, little clusters of homes or mobile homes, and perhaps some tobacco fields. It's OK for a break but quickly becomes about as boring as the more direct approach on Highway 17.

One interesting stop, right on the highway shortly after you leave Wilmington, is the **Poplar Grove Plantation.** It has an unusual history in that it not only survived the Civil War, but it became economically successful again by growing peanuts. The original plantation operated in the tradition of the times, as a self-supporting agricultural community with more than sixty slaves. The manor house burned down in 1849 and was rebuilt the following year where it now stands. When you visit the plantation, guides in period costume lead you on a tour of the manor house—a three-floor Greek-revival style building—and the outbuildings, describing what daily life on the plantation was like. In the manor house you can inspect displays of period furniture, clothes, and artifacts. The outbuildings include a tenant house, smokehouse, herb cellar, kitchen (plantation kitchens were always in separate buildings), blacksmith shop, and a turpentine and saltworks display. With or without a guide, looking at these buildings dramatically brings home some realities of history. A visitor looking at the small, roughly finished, uninsulated tenant house said, "It's hard to imagine that a whole family actually lived in here." Another visitor, seeing the mock hams, sausages, and bacons hanging in the smokehouse, wondered what the real thing would have been like in such hot weather and said, "It's a wonder everybody didn't die of food poisoning."

For children, Poplar Grove Plantation has lots of open spaces, shaded with live oaks, sycamores, and magnolias, for running; a playground; and some farm animals they can see and maybe even touch.

The manor house restaurant serves good southern cooking and vegetables that aren't cooked until you place your order. Much of the produce is local, and often one of the cooks or another will boast that the squash or okra is from her husband's garden. Lunches, which include such homey basics as beef stew, fried okra, squash, and, of course, peanut butter pie, are served in the lower area, which you enter through a door under the porch stairs in the back of the house. You can also order quiches, salads, burgers, and sandwiches. Prices begin as low as $3.50.

Dinner, for which you need a reservation except on Thursdays, is served in an attractive dining room on the second floor where crystal chandeliers and lace curtains set the tone. The evening menu includes a variety of fresh seafood and such other possibilities as Filet Wellington, Chicken Grand Marnier, and Quail aux Pruneau. Prices range from about $10 to $25. Beer and wine but not hard liquor are available.

A modest fee is charged for the house tour. Visitors may walk around the plantation for free. The plantation is open February through December from 9:00 A.M. to 5:00 P.M., Monday through Saturday, and from noon to 5:00 P.M., Sunday. The restaurant serves lunch from 11:30 A.M. to 2:30 P.M. Evening restaurant hours by reservation (919-686-9518—business office, 919-686-9503—restaurant).

Continuing north on Highway 17 takes you through some very local, un-touristy areas, such as Holly Ridge, where the mayor's office is also the office of Ocean Aire Realty. If you want more of a sense of the area, shortly after you pass Holly Ridge turn left on Verona Road, and following the signs jog toward Haws Run. You'll go by some pretty little houses with lovingly tended gardens, then an abandoned trailer park, and finally many occupied mobile homes on the way back out to Highway 17. This detour of only a few miles gives a view of what many small North Carolina communities near the coast are like.

Then you're into the area around Jacksonville, which is shaped and colored by Camp Lejeune Marine Base. Traffic is fairly heavy, and the area bulges with the kind of commercial development that surrounds military bases: motels, restaurants, amusements, shopping centers, and the like. But even though driving through such a section isn't as relaxing as spinning along a country road, it's tremendously instructive and sometimes funny. Most of the people you see in most of the vehicles are heartbreakingly young men with habitually perfect posture and haircuts so short you can almost see their scalps from the next automobile. Often they're in pairs or groups, and often they're towing boats or hauling bikes. The progression of the establishments and signs they pass along the road tell a story: Foxy Lady, New Ink Tattoo Shop, Luigi's (where you can get a remarkably good Italian meal), a motel sign "Welcome Mr. Nunnery," Real Value Diamond Outlet, an assortment of churches, and The Maternity and Newborn Store.

Here's information of a more dignified nature. Camp Lejeune is one of the most complete training centers in the world and covers 110,000 acres. You may wish to stop at the Beirut Memorial, honoring those killed in Beirut and Grenada. It is outside the gate of Camp Johnson on Highway 24. You can't get onto the base without a pass, and you can't get a pass without a driver's license and registration certificate. The information center at the main gate on Highway 24 is open twenty-four hours a day (919–451–2197).

From Jacksonville, you could logically continue up Highway 17 to New Bern, or you could travel east on Highway 24 toward the ocean to check out the Bogue Banks and then go on to Morehead City, Beaufort, and Atlantic, and ferry across to the Outer Banks. Better yet, if you're not hurrying, avoid this section of Highway 24, which runs along another edge of the Marine base, and continue north about 15 miles more on Highway 17, where you pick up Highway 58, which runs southeast along the side of the Croatan National Forest and is a much more pleasant drive to the coast. **Cedar Point** is a nice place to stop for a picnic or a rest and perhaps a hike along the Cedar Point Tideland Trail. You'll find camping areas and picnic tables in the shade along the water. Nearby is Cape Carteret, a little town that's probably completely solved its crime problem by locating its ABC (liquor) store right next to the police and town hall offices.

Aside from learning that Emerald Island is a sea turtle sanctuary, you're probably not going to find much that pleases you driving over to the Bogue Banks. The entire barrier island, which is nearly 30 miles long, has been developed commercially to the point where condos, cottages, and water slides line the beaches, and beach shops crowd one another along the highway. You may prefer to skip the Bogue Banks, stay on the mainland,

and head for Beaufort. But if at supper time you're in Cape Carteret on Highway 58 a mile north of the intersection of Highway 24, stop at **Meko's Restaurant,** an Italian seafood restaurant at the Emerald Isle Bridge. The restaurant has been in the same family for three generations; the proprietor is named Bertha; everything that can be homemade is homemade; seafood is never fried. Bertha goes to the local docks every afternoon to select the seafood. Some of us would drive half a day to find a restaurant like that. Probably the crab cakes and soft-shell crabs are Meko's most spectacular specialties. Prices begin at about $6 for pasta dishes and go to only about $13 for the most expensive seafood entree. Dress is casual, since the restaurant caters to the beach crowd. It opens seven days a week at 5:00 P.M. (919-393-6444).

Off the Beaten Path in The Northern Coast and Islands

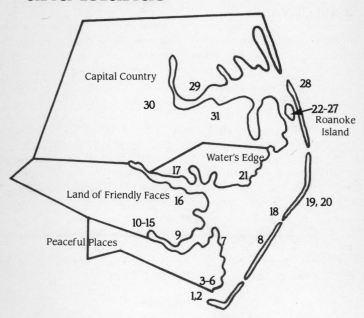

Capital Country

29

30

31

28

22-27
Roanoke
Island

Water's Edge

17

21

Land of Friendly Faces

16

19, 20

10-15

18

9

Peaceful Places

7

8

3-6

1,2

1. Morehead City
2. Bogue's Pocket Cafe
3. Beaufort
4. Old Town Beaufort
   Restoration Tour
5. North Carolina
   Maritime Museum
6. Landgon House
7. Morris Marina
8. Portsmouth Island
9. Oriental
10. New Bern
11. Tryon Palace
12. Harmony House Inn
13. The Henderson House
14. Fireman's Museum
15. Bank of the Arts
16. Aurora Fossil Museum

17. Bath
18. Ocracoke
19. Oscar's House
20. The Back Porch
21. Mettamuskeet National
    Wildlife Refuge
22. Fort Raleigh National
    Historic Site
23. *Elizabeth II* State Historic Site
24. Scarborough Inn
25. Clara's Seafood Grill
26. Tranquil House Inn
27. Fisherman's Wharf Restaurant
28. Wright Brothers National
    Memorial
29. The Lords Proprietors' Inn
30. Hope Plantation
31. Somerset Place

The Northern Coast and Islands

Peaceful Places

Your next major stop as you head north along the coast is **Morehead City,** a deep port where the Intracoastal Waterway joins the Atlantic Ocean. It is both a commercial fishing town and a summer resort area, appealing especially to sport fishers. The waterfront is more devoted to commerce than tourism, has more than 5,000 square feet of continuous wharf, and includes a lot of shipping storage space. That means the waterfront isn't really pretty; it's too commercial and busy, but the activity is authentic and interesting. As a traveler, if you aren't here to fish, you're probably here to eat fish. The area has plenty of moderately priced motels and more seafood restaurants than you could patronize in two weeks' hard eating. If you ask people where to go, they'll most often make the unlikely sounding recommendation of the Sanitary Fish Market Restaurant (919-247-3111). It's just a block from Highway 70, on Bogue Sound. This is a big, casual, family-oriented place that seats more than 600 people and serves all kinds of seafood and no alcohol. It has been owned and operated by the same family for more than fifty years. Open 11:00 A.M. to 9:00 P.M. daily. Closed in December.

If you say you don't want to go where everybody goes but want to eat at a place only a special few know about, you'll probably end up at the **Bogue's Pocket Cafe.** The proprietors of this newish restaurant, at 715 Evans Street, are Caroline Robinson and Martha Bourne. Martha sums up the difference between the Bogue's Pocket Cafe and the majority of other local seafood restaurants metaphorically. "We don't serve hush puppies." Also, the place is comparatively small, seating about sixty people at most. The menu changes weekly, depending on what is available at the docks for its inspiration. "What we prepare is always fresh and local," Martha says. She prefers grilling, baking, and sautéing to deep-frying. The bread and desserts are homemade. One of the most popular desserts recently has been the chocolate Grand Marnier cake, the kind of dessert you might as well just pat directly onto your hips. Beer and wine are available. Dress is casual. Given the restaurant's exterior, it almost has to be. Can you seriously picture dressing to the teeth to go into a green cinder-block building with purple stripes? As an innkeeper in Beaufort who often sends guests to the Bogue Pocket Cafe said, "It's strange to look at, but the food is out of this world." In the summer the restaurant is open daily 11:00 A.M. to 2:00 P.M. for lunch and 6:00 to 10:00 P.M. for dinner. In the off-season the restaurant is open the same hours Tuesday through Saturday. Reservations are not accepted. Occasionally during slow times, the proprietors will close to take a week off, so if you're traveling in the off-season, it's a good idea to call ahead (919-247-5351).

From Morehead City it's just a short drive over the Paul Graydon Bridge to **Beaufort,** a picture-book quaint village that was once a fishing village and is now a low-key vacation spot. And learn to say it right. Everyone in town will correct you if you say Bewfort because that's a coastal village in South Carolina. The good place, in North Carolina, is Boefort.

It's the kind of place that makes vacationers go home and dump well-established jobs so that they can return to Beaufort as innkeepers or restaurateurs. The area was settled more than 275 years ago by French Huguenots and English sailors. The little port saw heavy use during the American Revolution, the War of 1812, and the Civil War. Perhaps the concentration of so much history in so small an area gave an extra boost here to the nationwide enthusiasm for historic preservation generated by the country's bicentennial. At any rate, in less than twenty years, Beaufort has managed an impressive restoration of many eighteenth-century homes, shops, and even the jail. Much of this you can appreciate just wandering around town and staying at the bed and breakfast houses in one of the old homes. For more formal instruction, pick up a self-guided walking-tour map at the 1825 Josiah Bell House, or take the **Old Town Beaufort Restoration Tour** from the same location. In addition to the old homes, jail, and courthouse, the tour includes the apothecary shop, which gives you a slightly gory look at the medical products and practices of the eighteenth century. Tour rates are modest. Tours available Monday through Saturday, 9:30 A.M. to 3:30 P.M. (919-728-5225).

Plan also to spend time in the **North Carolina Maritime Museum** (315 Front Street). The museum contains artifacts related to everything from fish and fossils to ships, as well as aquariums, pictures, and books. If you enjoy miniatures, you'll be impressed with the museum's model-ship collection. In addition to the displays, the museum offers a variety of guided field trips focusing on wildflowers, birds, fossils, and so on. There are even classes in boat building. Admission free. Open Monday through Friday, 9:00 A.M. to 5:00 P.M.; Saturday, 10:00 A.M. to 5:00 P.M.; and Sunday, 1:00 to 5:00 P.M. (919-728-7317). For a schedule of special events that could affect your travel plans, write the museum at 315 Front Street, Beaufort, 28516.

Of the several bed and breakfast establishments you might choose, **Langdon House,** at 123 Craven Street (919-728-5499), is especially congenial. This colonial home, built in 1732, is the oldest building in Beaufort operated as a bed and breakfast. All four rooms have private baths and queen-size beds. Two porches, one on the first and another on the second floor, invite people watching, stargazing, and woolgathering. Breakfast is a full show—no soggy doughnuts in a box with coffee in Styrofoam cups here. Some mornings, for instance, it's orange pecan waffles with orange butter.

Part of the establishment's charm comes from the antiques, including paintings and musical instruments that earlier residents of the building have donated in the interests of the restoration's authenticity. A bigger attraction yet is the congeniality of the people. Jimm Prest knows the area intimately and likes to talk about it; Lynn Monteleone can describe people, houses, and restaurants so graphically that her words bring full-blown images to your mind. And you feel that she's enjoying the conversation. Incidentally, one of the places they like to recommend for dinner is the Bogue Pocket Cafe in Morehead City. For people who hate to get back in the car once they've settled in, the Net House, a short walk away on Turner Street, serves broiled or lightly battered and fried seafood. As Lynn says, "You'll know when you're there because it's got a big red crab in front."

Langdon House cooperates in handling overflow and referring extra guests with the Captain's Quarters, a bed and breakfast in a Victorian house at 315 Ann Street (919-728-7711). Captain Dick and Ruby Collins like to chat. Captain Dick's title comes not from the sea, as you might suppose, but from his days as an airline pilot. When you appear for your continental breakfast, he says, "Top o' the mornin' to ya!"

One could stay in Beaufort a long time just wandering around, eating seafood, and sitting on the porch reading trashy novels. Assuming you want to see more, however, you should push on north almost to the end of Highway 70 east, to the little town of Atlantic (not to be confused with Atlantic Beach), where you can catch the ferry to the Outer Banks. Actually, you can't catch it; you're going to have to call ahead and arrange this part of your trip carefully. At **Morris Marina,** Don and Katie Morris run their private ferry business taking sightseers and fishers to various sites along the islands of Outer Banks. Don can tell stories of these places for about as long as you want to listen.

In particular, visit **Portsmouth Island.** It's uninhabited now, but 635 people once lived on the 30-mile-long island in the village of Portsmouth. Ultimately, they couldn't survive the weather, especially hurricanes. A particularly bad one in 1846 opened Hatteras and Oregon inlets and changed shipping patterns, which cut off future economic development for the village. Gradually, the people left, first the young and then the old. According to Joel Arrington, writing in the magazine *Wildlife in North Carolina,* only fourteen people remained on the island in 1950; the last male resident died in 1971, after which the last two women gave up and moved to the mainland. The buildings of the village remain a little beat up but intact, maintained by the U.S. Park Service.

Your difficulty in seeing the village will be that even after you've ferried across to the island, you need a four-wheel-drive vehicle to travel the 18 miles up the beach from the ferry landing to get to the village, because there are no roads. But getting a ride in a four-wheel-drive vehicle in North Carolina isn't as hard as it sounds. They are ubiquitous, especially among sportsmen (and it's not sexist to leave out women here, for there are few). Enough such people like to visit the village that by planning ahead with Don Morris you should be able to arrange a ride if you don't have a four-wheeler of your own. Indeed, the sight of half a dozen or so men in fishing clothes, sitting quietly on the benches inside the old, weathered, and abandoned Portsmouth Village Methodist Church when they're supposed to be at water's edge fishing may be as special an experience as visiting the village. This isn't a likely place to lodge. A few cabins, locally known as "hooches," are rented, but during peak fishing seasons they're reserved as much as two years ahead of time. Still, if you'd like to try some truly primitive conditions on the island, it doesn't hurt to ask. For information about ferry hours and renting hooches, write Morris

Marina at Star Route Box 761, Atlantic, 28511, or phone (919) 225-4261.

A simpler way to visit the village, though less colorful and a bit more *on* the beaten (or should it be rowed, in this case?) path, is to take a ferry from Ocracoke Island that brings you directly to the spot. You need to arrange in advance. Phone Rudy Austin (919-928-4363 or 919-928-4281) or Dave McLawhorn (919-928-5921). The more people you can round up to make the trip with you, the less it costs. It's $40 for two round trip, but only $15 per person when you have three or more.

Another ferry leaves from Harker's at about $10 per person. The schedule varies (919-728-3866). If you're not sure how to manage the trip and would like more information and advice, the National Park Service, 415 Front Street, Beaufort 28516, is tremendously helpful and enthusiastic (919-728-2121).

Land of Friendly Faces

The entire area along the northern coast, the barrier islands, and the Outer Banks is a maze of toll ferries, free ferries, private ferries, and bridges. The way you organize your trips here depends on everything from the weather to how much time you want to spend driving or being ferried. Remember that a ferry is not a fast way to travel. In planning trips in this area, sometimes it works better to find a pleasant base to which you return after each foray in a new direction. Try New Bern as a slightly inland base from which, one way or another, you can get to a wonderful variety of places to spend a day or so. Everyone in New Bern will have ideas for you, which will certainly include **Oriental.**

Oriental is about 25 miles east of New Bern on Highway 55. It has won a reputation as the sailing capital of the East Coast and almost always has a sailing school or camp in process. Except for a couple of antiques shops, a modest motel or two, and some simple restaurants, there's not much here except nice people. If you want to spend a night at a bed and breakfast here, the Tar Heel Inn at Oriental at 205 Church Street (919-249-1078) has six rooms with private baths, king- and queen-size beds, and handicap facilities. The inn was built at the turn of the century and has been restored to duplicate the feel of an English country inn—with contemporary amenities. The innkeepers, Dave and Patti Nelson, serve a big breakfast.

Then again, once you're in **New Bern** you may not want to go anywhere else at all, not just because there's so much to see and do but also because this is one of the friendliest towns anywhere. To give you an idea, a couple staying at a bed and breakfast inn in the historic district was walking to a nearby restaurant where they had dinner reservations when they stopped to admire an especially nicely restored house. The owners, who happened to be on the porch, invited the couple in for a drink and showed them around. They spent so much time chatting that the couple never did make it to the restaurant.

On the outside chance that you might not be so generously befriended by strangers, stop in the tourist center at the chamber of commerce about two blocks from Highway 70, near the Trent River at the end of Middle Street, when you get to town. Signs point the way from all major entrances. Everyone here is extraordinarily friendly too. One middle-aged travel writer who stopped in for maps and directions struck up a conversation with a teenaged summer assistant. They've been corresponding ever since.

If you're an antiquer, be sure to get a copy of the brochure "Antique Shops of New Bern," which gives particulars on more than a dozen antiques shops, complete with a map and an explanation of American furniture styles from Queen Anne style (1725-1750) through the arts and crafts and mission styles of the early 1900s.

You'll also be able to pick up full details on **Tryon Palace** Restorations and Garden Complex, where first a royal government and then an independent state government were housed. In colonial times Tryon Palace was known as the most beautiful building in America. The elaborate formal gardens as well as the elegant buildings and furnishings have been restored.

Tours conducted by guides in costume lead you through the rooms; give you a look at demonstrations of candle making, cloth making, cooking, and other period activities; and fill you in on specific facts about the buildings and their earlier, illustrious occupants. If you just want to tour the gardens, you can take a self-guided tour. The complex (919-638-1560) is open year-round, Monday through Saturday, 9:30 A.M. to 4:00 P.M., and Sunday from 1:30 to 4:00 P.M. Closed Thanksgiving Day, December 24-26, and January 1. Moderate rates. Write Tryon Palace, Box 1007, New Bern 28560.

An interesting and historical yet cheery and comfortable place to stay in New Bern is **Harmony House Inn,** 215 Pollock Street (919-636-3810). Buzz and Diane Hansen, the proprietors, bring to innkeeping the kind of personable warmth that makes business travelers who stay there regularly feel free to stop in unannounced, use the phone in the inn's office, and then hurry out to the car, saying they'll be back to spend the night on the way through tomorrow.

The story of the house is complex and deserves Diane's telling, but here's a teaser. The house began as a four-room, two-story home with Greek Revival styling. As the family grew, the house was enlarged; then around the turn of the century, as the children grew older, two sons wanted the house, so it was sawed in half, and one side was moved 9 feet away from the other. A huge hallway and another set of stairs were put in to join the building yet divide it into two separate dwellings. Now the two hallways, front doors, and sitting areas are all part of the inn. It's furnished with antiques, reproductions created by local craftspeople, and family memorabilia, mainly from Diane's family. A delight in the parlor is the 1875 organ, in such perfect working order that Buzz easily plays for you without missing a note. Breakfast is always an extravaganza, including eggs, cheese, meat, cereal, and fruit.

After a day of touring, you can rest awhile at the Harmony House Inn and then walk to dinner. **The Henderson House,** right across the street at 216 Pollock (919-673-4784), has been serving fine meals for nearly twenty years. The atmosphere is elegant. Guests are invited to tour an art gallery on the second floor where the paintings of Robert Weaver, an internationally known artist and the chef's father, are displayed. Dining specialties include southern peanut soup and cold apricot soup, as well as a seafood casserole, scallops, lobster, lamb, veal, and chicken entrees. For lunch Henderson House offers such delights as broiled crabmeat on English muffin and Fruits de Mer en Croute. All spirits are available. As you'd expect, all the desserts are homemade. Everything is delicious, the kind of dining guests at the bed and breakfasts talk about over breakfast the next morning. Also as you'd expect, the prices are not inexpensive. Lunch is served from 11:00 A.M. to 2:00 P.M., dinner from 6:00 to 9:00 P.M.

For a more casual, less expensive dinner, also within walking distance of Harmony House Inn, try Federal Alley at 235 Craven Street. The atmosphere is typified by old brick, young waiters and waitresses, lots of green plants, colorful international flags, and a menu ranging from seafood to beef, served with potato, salad, and vegetable. The salad bar is set up in an old ice-filled claw-foot bathtub. The restaurant has a small bar and lounge area. Open Monday through Saturday, 11:30 A.M. to 10:00 P.M.

On a day when you haven't put all your energy into touring the palace, you might check out three small, less well-known museums, each within walking distance of the other.

The Attmore-Oliver House Museum, built in 1790, at 511 Broad Street (parking at 510 Pollock Street), belonged at one time to Samuel Chapman, who had earlier been a first lieutenant under General George Washington. It features eighteenth- and nineteenth-century antiques, artifacts related to New Bern's history, and a Civil War museum room. There's also a collection of eighteenth-century dolls. Open Tuesday through Saturday, 1:00 to 4:30 P.M. (919-638-8558). Closed two winter months. Modest fee.

Fireman's Museum, across the corner at 411 Hancock Street, houses a collection of memorabilia of North Carolina's earliest fire company, from 1845, and of the Button Company, a rival volunteer company. The museum guide himself is a volunteer fireman of many years. The displays include early steamers and pump wagons, large photographs, and the mounted head of an old fire horse named Fred, who, at least according to publicists, died in harness answering a false alarm in 1925. No information is offered about what happened to the rest of the horse. Open Tuesday through Saturday, 9:30 A.M. to noon, and 1:00 to 5:00 P.M.; Sunday, 1:00 to 5:00 P.M. Modest fee.

At **Bank of the Arts,** 317 Middle Street (919-638-2577), about a block away, you'll find artists' exhibits in sculpture, oil, watercolor, pottery, and photography. The exhibits change every month. Originally a neoclassical bank building, it is now home of the Craven Arts Council and Gallery. The gallery has 30-foot-high ceilings with ornate colored plaster in the beaux arts style. Sometimes afternoon concerts, storytellers, and folksingers are offered. Open weekdays, 10:00 A.M. to 4:00 P.M., and Saturday, 11:00 A.M. to 3:00 P.M. Closed Sunday. Admission free.

In a town as historically significant as New Bern, you could easily get into more historical data than you really want on a vacation, but to enjoy the area you should know at least a few basic facts. The community was first settled in 1710, by Swiss and German immigrants, who named it for Bern, Switzerland. It was capital of the colonies from 1766 to 1776 and then state capital. Economically, the area flourished mostly because of its port at the time of the Revolution, slumped during the Civil War, then recovered fairly quickly. From about the time of World War II, it has restored gradually its historical spots and become a comfortably established, low-key attraction. Irrelevant but fun to know: Pepsi-Cola was invented here, but the guy went bankrupt during a sugar scarcity; and the official New Bern shrub is *Lagerstroemia*—crepe myrtle. The brilliant blossoms brighten most streets and home landscapes many months of the year.

Water's Edge

One interesting trip from New Bern is the drive north on Highway 17 to Washington, where you pick up Highway 264 to Bath, Belhaven, and Swan Quarter. The trip winds through mostly rural areas, although just north of New Bern on Highway 17 you'll come to a business area where you can buy supplies. Stop at the Eagle Supermarket, which is a lot more fun and will give you a much better sense of the local population than the little convenience stores along the way. Out front everything from bales of straw to wheelbarrows is stacked along the windows. Inside are all the standard grocery store offerings plus some of the friendliest local employees you'll ever meet. The store is open from 7:00 A.M. to 9:00 P.M., Monday through Saturday, and from 8:00 A.M. to 9:00 P.M., Sunday.

You'll find more local color just before you come to Washington, at Chocowinity, billed as "Home of the Indians," where the high school boasts having won a series of state and regional girls basketball titles and cheerleading championships, beginning in 1980. It's all detailed proudly on a huge sign in front of the school. Around the corner on Highway 33 west, L Cheapos Flea Market and Scotts Collectibles and Antiques stand side by side, with old furniture, knickknacks, and odds and ends packed inside, jammed into the windows, and overflowing out onto the sidewalks. These aren't the kinds of places where you expect operating hours to remain unchanged month to month, but if you happen by when the establishments are open, you can have a lot of fun browsing, chatting, and maybe making an honest-to-goodness find. Chocowinity is a crossroads community, not set up to lure or serve tourists, so don't count on it as a place to stop, fuel up, eat, and so on. Look at it as an absolutely honest glimpse of small-town coastal North Carolina.

From here you can drive on through Washington to Bath or get to Bath by crossing the Pamlico River on the ferry, which you approach by following Highway 33 east from Chocowinity through corn and tobacco country, past a brick house with a stonework chimney that's bigger than the house, past Possum Track Road and on to Aurora—a drive of about 33 miles. This route actually backtracks some, and you could get to Aurora faster by taking State Road 1003 from Highway 17 just outside New Bern, but then you'd miss Chocowinity. It all depends on how much exploring you want to do.

If you're interested in fossils, especially fish fossils from the Pliocene period, be sure to take time in Aurora to visit the **Aurora Fossil Museum** on Main Street (919-322-4238). Margaret McMicken, who lives right there in town, is in charge of the museum, but she's the only employee, so if she has a doctor's appointment or wants lunch or needs to attend a tourism meeting, she closes the museum during her absence. If you're coming from a distance, be sure to call ahead. Should you get there at a time when the museum is closed, you are welcome to scavenge through the piles of rejects across the street from the museum to gather your own fossils. Usual hours are from 9:00 A.M. to 4:30 P.M., Monday through Friday, and by appointment. Admission free.

A mile or so outside Aurora, Highway 306 north turns left, bringing you to Keith Brantley's service station, the kind of place where some of the local old-timers sit around inside and talk about the weather, where whoever pumps your gas actually cleans your windshield, and where you need a key and a good kick on the door to get into the rest room. Across the road, Brunches Restaurant serves mostly fast food without the franchise chain atmosphere and offers excellent iced tea. The restaurant is open from 5:30 A.M. to 8:00 P.M. daily. From there Highway 306 north goes about 7 miles to the Pamlico River Ferry, which is free; the crossing takes about twenty-five minutes. From the ferry landing, go left on Highway 92 into historic **Bath,** where you come first to the visitor center.

Bath is the kind of place you fantasize about when you dream of leaving the rat race for a simpler way of life. The town, with a population not much over two hundred, only 3 blocks long and 2 wide, is friendly and without guile; people cutting their grass or working in their gardens wave as you walk or drive by. They're proud of their history but see it with enough humor to name the state liquor store "Ye Olde ABC Package Store."

The folks in the Historic Bath Visitor Center encourage you to see the twenty-five-minute orientation film, "A Town Called Bath," before you begin a self-guided walking tour or take one of the guided tours. These begin on the hour and half-hour, from 9:00 A.M. to 5:00 P.M., Monday through Saturday, and from 1:00 to 5:00 P.M., Sunday. They take about an hour and a half. Modest admission charged.

You can approach the history a couple different ways. Bath was the home of Blackbeard the pirate, and some of his loot is still supposed to be buried somewhere in the area. It's also the oldest incorporated town in North Carolina. The Palmer-Marsh House, from the colonial period, dates back to about 1740. The St. Thomas Church, which was begun in 1734, is the oldest church in the state. It has been restored and is still used by the Episcopal Diocese as an active place of worship, though visitors are allowed to come in anytime for a self-guided tour. The St. Thomas parish had a collection in the early 1700s of more than 1,000 books and pamphlets from England, and that collection became the first public library in North Carolina.

While you can easily take in the tours in less than a day, if you'd like to hang around to sample the pace of Bath, you could stay at the Bath Guest House on South Main Street (919-923-6811). The place is operated by Paul and Irene Komarow. A 60-foot window offers a breathtaking view of the water, and in addition to a full breakfast, staying here entitles you to use the Komarows' sailboats, canoes, rowboats, and bicycles (including a bicycle built for two). Paul says he'd sell the business if someone offered him enough money—about half a million dollars—but he doesn't really expect it to happen. Still, if you've got your heart set on overnighting in Bath, call ahead and make sure that Paul, or his successor, is still there.

From Bath, it's a pretty drive of 11 miles on Highway 99 to Belhaven, where you pick up Highway 264 east, crossing the Intracoastal Waterway to Swan Quarter. Most of this distance is lovely, although you'll probably see a lot of heavy equipment in some areas. In early summer, hibiscus bushes bloom along the road, red and yellow cannas adorn the lawns of farmhouses and mobile homes, and apple trees bear so heavily that the fruits seem to be dripping from the laden and drooping branches.

At Swan Quarter you can either take the ferry to Ocracoke,

probably the best known of the barrier islands, or you can continue driving up the coast along Highway 264 to Manns Harbor, where you drive across the bridge to Roanoke Island and on over the Outer Banks islands. If you plan to take the ferry, a two-and-one-half-hour ride, call the Ocracoke Visitor Center (919-928-4531) ahead of time to check on current schedules and weather conditions.

Ocracoke, an old fishing village, is fun if you're willing to take a couple of days and just hang out; if all you do is drive through, you've missed most of what it has to offer. Of course there's history. As early as 1715, Ocracoke was a port of the North Carolina colony, where Blackbeard the pirate buried his treasure and lost his head. The head got carried off to Bath; presumably the treasure's still somewhere on the island. These days, fishing, bicycling (you can rent bicycles here), and bird hunting are bigger attractions than treasure hunting. But mostly Ocracoke is a place to escape the chrome-and-plastic world of commercial tourism. You can enjoy the remnants of Old English lilting in the speech of some of the old-timers as you walk around the village, read up on local history and nature, and visit the famous pony pens where the remaining descendants of the famous Spanish mustangs are protected. For full information about the island, ferries, and the marina, contact the Ocracoke Visitor Center (919-928-4731) or the Outer Banks Chamber of Commerce, P.O. Box 1757, Kill Devil Hills 27948 (phone 919-441-8144.)

The island has several motels and some bed and breakfast inns. One of the nicest is also one of the smallest. **Oscar's House** is run by Ann Ehringhaus, whose father, Oscar, the lighthouse keeper and builder, once lived in it. The house is furnished in a style that Ann calls "comfortable and artistic." A professional photographer, she has traded some of her work with other artists, acquiring baskets, pottery, watercolors, and photographs, all of which enliven the mellow, tongue-in-groove pine walls of the house. And, as Ann says, "You can sit in the furniture. No delicate Victorian antiques."

Ann's full breakfasts feature produce from her organic garden and include everything from fresh fish to shrimp creole. It's the kind of breakfast that allows people to skip lunch. If you'd like something low-fat, vegetarian, macrobiotic, or otherwise special, Ann will accommodate you. "Cooking is my favorite part of the B&B business," she says.

A big part of the charm of staying here is getting to know Ann, who knows the island and its residents intimately. Her book, *Ocracoke Portrait,* a collection of her photographs captioned with quotations from the islanders, is an understated, elegant picture of life on the island. The inn (919-928-1311, P.O. Box 206, Ocracoke, 27960) is open April through October. Special cooking workshops and photography workshops are sometimes scheduled at the beginning and end of the season.

Of the several small restaurants on the island, **The Back Porch,** in a shady area a half-mile north of the ferry terminal on Highway 1324, seems just right. The dining room is wood paneled, with a screened-in porch. The food is fresh, not prepared ahead, with homemade bread and desserts and subtle flavors of herb and spice that you can taste because the food isn't fried. Open daily from 5:00 to 10:00 P.M., April through November.

No matter how much you like it, sooner or later you'll have to leave Ocracoke. It's possible to drive on up the Outer Banks, but it's monotonous in some undeveloped areas, full of traffic elsewhere, and generally just not as interesting as you'd expect it to be. You might do better to ferry back across to Swan Quarter and drive from there north on Highway 264, toward Manns Harbor, where the bridge takes you across to Manteo on Roanoke Island. This trip takes you into the **Mattamuskeet National Wildlife Refuge,** a breathtaking wilderness of 50,000 acres comprising Lake Mattamuskeet, marshland, timber, and cropland. The lake is 18 miles long and about 6 miles wide, the largest natural lake in North Carolina.

In parts of the acreage, water levels are controlled mechanically to allow local farmers to plant corn and soybeans and to allow for overseeding some acres to provide food for the wildlife. The wooded areas along the boundaries of the refuge contain pine and mixed hardwoods. Some commercial logging and controlled burning are used to keep the woodlands healthy.

Headquarters for the refuge is off Highway 94, one and one-half miles north of Highway 264, between Swan Quarter and Englehard. Stopping in is a good way to learn all the possibilities of the place. At various points you can crab, fish in fresh or salt water, and hunt. The area begs for bird watching, photographing, and painting. Depending on the time of year, you might spot swans, Canada geese, song and marsh birds, and even bald eagles, as well as deer, bobcats, and river otter.

But this is a refuge administered by the U.S. Fish and Wildlife Service of the Department of the Interior and operates by their rules. You can't camp, swim, or collect exotic plants here. There are restrictions on firearms. The refuge is open from 5:00 A.M. to 9:00 P.M. daily. For full details on how to enjoy the place and lists of lodgings available nearby, write Refuge Manager, Mattamuskeet National Wildlife Refuge, Route 1, Box N-2, Swan Quarter, 27885.

When you're in the area, it's fun to gas up at the Matta-muskeet Sportsman's Center on Highway 264, where a long-bearded proprietor and his little kids dispense information, advice, directions, and such necessities as fishing and hunting equipment, bait shrimp, worms, ice, candy, beer, and soda. Oh, yes, and food.

From Mattamuskeet Lake, Highway 264 continues through lonely marsh and woodland up to Manns Harbor and across to Roanoke Island. The main community here, Manteo, used to be a small resort area. It's growing now, not excessively, but too much to suit the longtime residents who remember when the road through town didn't turn into bumper-to-bumper ribbons of automobiles during rush hour.

Roanoke Island

You'll remember from your grade-school history lessons that Roanoke Island is where the English first tried to establish a colony in the New World in 1585, encouraged by Queen Elizabeth I and led by Sir Walter Raleigh. They named it for Raleigh but couldn't keep it going. A year later those who had survived returned to England. In 1857, Raleigh tried again, this time including women and children in the group led by John White. Virginia Dare was born here. Then Sir Walter went sailing away for supplies. By the time he got back, three years later, the colony had vanished, leaving no signs of what might have happened to it. The **Fort Raleigh National Historic Site** memorializes the lost colony with a restoration of the old fort and a granite marker commemorating Virginia Dare's birth as the first English child born here. From June through August, the drama *The Lost Colony*, performed outdoors at the Waterford Theatre on the site, tells the story. One of Andy Griffith's acting roles in his pre-Mayberry years was as Sir Walter Raleigh in this show. Moderate admission charged. Phone (919) 473-3414 for exact schedules.

Next to the theater, The Elizabethan Gardens, created by the Garden Club of North Carolina as a memorial to the lost colonists, bloom from spring until fall, with roses, crepe myrtle, lilies, hydrangeas, and summer annuals. The garden features an extensive collection of old garden ornaments, some dating back to the time of the first Queen Elizabeth, as well as a sunken garden, a wildflower garden, an herb garden, and camelias and azaleas in season. Open from 9:00 A.M. to 8:00 P.M. daily. Closed Saturday and Sunday in December and January. Modest admission charged.

Complete your history lesson by visiting the *Elizabeth II* **State Historic Site,** across the bridge and opposite the Manteo waterfront. The museum (919-473-1144) contains exhibits depicting life in the sixteenth century, including a reproduction of a sailing vessel similar to what would have been used to bring the first colonists to Roanoke in 1585. A twenty-minute multimedia program gives you the feel of those early voyages and what it would have been like to live on the ship. In the summer, costumed actors portray early marines and colonists. After seeing the film, you may tour the ship. Open November 1 through March 31, 10:00 A.M. to 4:00 P.M., Tuesday through Sunday (last tour begins 3:00 P.M.). Closed Monday. Open April 1 through October 31, 10:00 A.M. to 6:00 P.M. daily (last tour begins at 5:00 P.M.). Write *Elizabeth II* State Historic Site, Manteo, 27954.

In downtown Manteo (named for an Indian of Roanoke who went back to England with the early sailors) on Highway 64/264, you can pick up a bit of local family history by staying at **Scarborough Inn** (919-473-3979), run by Phil and Sally Scarborough, longtime residents of the island. Six rooms in the inn and four in the annex are furnished with comfortable old furniture that has been in the family, or at least in the community, for generations. It's not fancy stuff but the kind of thing you remember from visiting old Aunt Lizzie or Great-grandma. Nearly every piece has a story that Phil and Sally, who love to talk, will tell you gladly. The rooms are simple but comfortable. Each has a private bath, a small refrigerator, and a coffee maker with coffee provided. No breakfast is served, but Sally leaves a couple packs of doughnuts by the coffee maker.

Across the road from Scarborough Inn, the Weeping Radish specializes in authentic German food served by waitresses in

Elizabeth II

Bavarian costume and accompanied by a variety of dark and light beers from the Weeping Radish microbrewery, all to the tune of Bavarian folk music. Open daily, 11:00 A.M. to 9:00 P.M. Tours of the brewery are available on a varying schedule (919-473-1991).

For more elegant accommodations and dining, try the Tranquil House Inn and **Clara's Seafood Grill,** both on the waterfront. According to Phil Scarborough, Clara's, in the waterfront condos overlooking rows of sailboats and yachts, makes the best crab cakes in town. Advertised on the menu as "more crab than cake," these hefty crab cakes are coated with a tempuralike batter that barely contains the large lumps of crab bursting from the cake. Homemade whole-wheat rolls, an imported beer or some wine, a house salad with strawberry vinaigrette, and a rich fudge Kentucky Derby pie complete a sumptuous meal, all for about $20. The atmosphere is up scale, but casual dress is appropriate. Clara's (919-473-8717) is in the condo division at the corner of Sir Walter Raleigh and Queen Elizabeth avenues. Open daily, 11:30 A.M. to 9:30 P.M. summer, and noon to 9:00 P.M. the rest of the year.

You might put what you don't spend at Clara's toward a special night at **Tranquil House Inn.** The inn, on the waterfront in downtown Manteo, whispers *luxury* when you enter—clearly a chocolates-on-the-pillow kind of place. The building is a reproduction of a typical nineteenth-century Outer Banks inn, with added contemporary conveniences a nineteenth-century traveler wouldn't even have dreamed about. Because of the pale cypress woodwork, glass, and stained glass throughout, the inn's interior seems almost as bright and sunny as the docks outside. On the first floor, in a little library with rockers and a leather couch, a gas-log fireplace will keep the chill at bay while you look out on Shallowbag Bay. In the guest rooms, you find not only the expected amenities such as television and telephone, but also Oriental carpets, fine furnishings, and hand-tiled bathrooms. Rates, commensurate with the luxurious atmosphere, include continental breakfast (919-473-1404).

The other community on Roanoke Island, Wanchese (named for another Indian who took off for England), doesn't seem to know it is surrounded by tourists. Most of the people of Wanchese fish for a living. Driving on Highway 345 south to the village, you pass modest homes—many with a boat in the yard—battered vans, worn pickups, and lots of churches, flowers, and pets. Signs in some of the yards invite you to buy hand-carved duck decoys, driftwood, wood crafts, and nursery plants. All the people you see in the community will talk to you pleasantly and seem to enjoy your watching them work on the docks.

Fisherman's Wharf Restaurant, a large, unpretentious restaurant on the wharf, surrounded by pilings, wild stands of Queen Anne's lace, and rolls of chicken wire, specializes in broiled and fried seafood and Wanchese crab cakes at modest prices. From your table you can watch the same fishing fleets that probably caught what you're eating. Sometimes broadcasts from a religious radio station drift through a speaker at the door. No alcohol is sold or permitted on the premises. Open noon to 9:00

P.M. Monday through Saturday, from mid-April through October.

Before you leave Roanoke Island, take time to visit this branch of the North Carolina Aquarium, about a mile north of Manteo, off Highway 64. Here you get a close-up view of live marine life, including sharks, eels, and sea turtles. A touch tank, as the name implies, lets you feel live crabs and starfish. Open Monday through Saturday, 9:00 A.M. to 5:00 P.M., and Sunday 1:00 to 5:00 P.M. The aquarium maintains a full calendar of special events, from seafood-cooking workshops to field trips and cruises. For a current schedule, write the aquarium, Roanoke Island, Manteo, 27954, or call (919) 473-3493.

From Manteo, a short drive across the bridge on Highway 64/264 takes you to Bodie Island (which isn't really an island anymore but a location along the northern section of the Outer Banks), where it's worth stopping to see the Bodie Island Lighthouse, operating since 1872. Aside from Coquina Beach, a good beach for swimming and fishing, you won't find many attractions here. A turn to the south, however, takes you to Hatteras Island, home of the tallest lighthouse in America, the Cape Hatteras Lighthouse. Although the lighthouse has been in place since 1869, erosion keeps eating away at the sand on which it's built, and the National Park Service is exploring possibilities for moving it or finding some other way of protecting it. This area is undeveloped because the protected Cape Hatteras National Seashore comprises Hatteras, some of the southern end of Bodie, and Ocracoke. Here you can see natural beaches and their attendant wildlife, seashells as they wash ashore and accumulate, and vegetation dwarfed and gnarled by salt and wind but not threatened by macadam, all without water slides. For more information on the area, write: Superintendent, Cape Hatteras National Seashore, Route 1, Box 675, Manteo, 27954, or call (919) 473-2111.

It's a different story turning north from Bodie Island. You drive through the kind of beach-strip conglomeration of motels, restaurants, gas stations, fast-food chains, and beach shops that typifies most popular beach areas. As a follower of unbeaten paths, you might choose to skip it, unless you're interested in seeing the **Wright Brothers National Memorial** at Kill Devil Hills, which marks the spot where Wilbur and Orville Wright first got off the ground in powered flight on December 7, 1903. The visitor

Cape Hatteras Lighthouse

center here has full-sized copies of the brothers' glider and their first plane. The brothers' workshop and living quarters have been re-created too. Open daily, 9:00 A.M. to 7:00 P.M. Winter hours may be shorter. Modest admission charged on weekends (919-441-7430).

Kill Devil Hills is a destination resort area, probably the kind of thing you're trying to avoid. But if it seems appropriate to spend the night, try Ye Olde Cherokee Inn Bed and Breakfast, a big pink beach house run by Bob and Phyllis Combs, self-described as "a couple of Yankees from Ohio who came south to get warm." The Combs bought the Cherokee, which was originally a hunting and fishing lodge, from a sea captain. The six guest rooms are done in cypress, with white ruffled curtains and ceiling fans. It might surprise the sea captain that the rooms have private baths and color television. The inn is open from April until October. Rates include a continental breakfast (919-441-6127).

Once you get this far north on the Outer Banks, it makes more sense to keep driving north on Highway 158 across the bridge onto the mainland than it does to backtrack. Following Highway 158, you can pick up Highway 17 south at Elizabeth City. Elizabeth City merits at least a brief stop, if only because it is at the site of a canal dug in 1790 with the unlikely name of Dismal Swamp Canal. A Coast Guard installation nearby and the local shipyard make this clearly a working, rather than a vacationing, area. The town, however, has a number of interesting historical buildings that are easy to check by taking a walking tour. For a map write the chamber of commerce, 502 E. Ehringhaus Street, P.O. Box 426, Elizabeth City, 27907, or call (919) 335-4365.

The Museum of the Albemarle (919-335-1453), about 3 miles south of town on Highway 17, provides information on the area, known as the Historic Albemarle Area, along with displays of artifacts and exhibits related to local history. (Colonists first revolted openly against the English monarchy here.) Open Tuesday through Saturday, 9:00 A.M. to 5:00 P.M., and Sunday, 2:00 to 5:00 P.M. Closed Monday and major holidays. Admission free.

The next community along Highway 17, Hertford, the Perquimans County seat (population only about 2,000) is on the Perquimans River, which feeds into Albemarle Sound. It's worth a stop to visit the Newbold-White House, believed to be the oldest house in North Carolina, probably built sometime between the early 1660s and 1685. The house has been restored, preserving much of the original handwork of the brick chimneys and walls and some of the woodwork. Though not the original, the furnishings are authentic pieces dating from the seventeenth century. Open March to Thanksgiving, Monday through Saturday, 10:00 A.M. to 4:30 P.M. Other times by appointment (919-426-7567). Modest admission charged.

As an alternate plan if you are pressed for time, you may decide to skip the northern Outer Banks and go back from Roanoke

Island on Highway 64, which takes you across the Alligator River and through the Alligator River Refuge (it's not clear whether the refuge protects people from alligators or the other way around) where you'll find lots of wildlife, picnic areas, and boating access. Either way, make your next stop Edenton, the first capital of colonial North Carolina. From Highway 64, take Highway 32 north. On Highway 17, keep going about 15 miles west from Hertford.

Capital Country

Although Edenton is in no way backward, it has managed to retain the calm and slower pace that we associate with earlier times and has done an outstanding job of preserving its historical sites and promulgating the facts.

Blackbeard lived here, even though he hung out in Bath and maybe left his treasure there. This would have been good pirate country. It was a busy port town in the eighteenth and early nineteenth centuries. During the revolutionary war, supplies were shipped from here to Washington's army farther north.

Edenton had some of the earliest female political activists too. In 1774, fifty-one women gathered in the courthouse square to sign a declaration vowing not to drink English tea or wear English clothing.

To steep yourself in colonial and revolutionary war history, you have a choice of a guided or a self-guided walking tour. Pick up a walking-tour map for a quarter, or join a guided tour for a modest fee at the Barker House Visitor Center. A free audiovisual presentation gives you some orientation in the area's history. The Barker house (c. 1782) was the home of Thomas Barker, a colonial agent in England, and his wife, Penelope, one of those ladies who boycotted English tea and clothing. Open Monday through Saturday, 10:00 A.M. to 4:30 P.M., and Sunday, 2:00 to 5:00 P.M. Closed Thanksgiving, Easter, December 24–26, and New Year's Day.

Because it's so pleasant, full of flowers, friendly people, and lovely waterfront vistas, spending the night in Edenton rests and relaxes you.

The Lords Proprietors' Inn, located at 300 North Broad Street (919-482-3641), has earned a reputation as one of the most elegant and gracious inns in the state. The inn comprises three separate restored homes in the historic district, grouped around lawn and gardens and the Whedbee House, on a brick patio, where continental breakfast is served. Each of the twenty rooms has private bath, cable television, videocassette player, and telephone. Arch and Jane Edwards, the proprietors, invite guests to use their swimming pool and to visit their private home, an authentically restored house of the 1800s. Also, they sponsor some weekend packages that include a tour of several private historic homes and a candlelight dinner.

All the guest rooms are light and airy. The common rooms have lots of open space, beautifully refinished old floors, and many whimsical decorating touches. You have the sense here of being in a professionally run inn of quality.

A few steps away, at 304 North Broad Street, Shack and Ruth Shackelford offer an entirely different lodging alternative. Governor Eden Inn (919–482–2072), four rooms with private bath and television in the old neoclassical family home, gives you the feeling of stopping in to spend the night with a friendly relative. Ruth and Shack are local folks who enjoy guests, like to serve tea on the balcony or downstairs verandah, and expect to sit in the parlor to chat with you. Shack enjoys a joke, or as Ruth puts it, "He's always cuttin' the fool," and Ruth is a homey soul whose conversations often begin, "Honey, let me tell you . . . "

As for places to eat when you're in town, you're in for a true off-the-beaten-path experience at Bob and Sharon's Bar-B-Que Barn on Highway 32 on the south side of town. For the most fun, sit at one of the five tables in the front rather than in the larger dining room in back. Up front, you can enjoy the company and comments of the local workers, such as the men from nearby Edenton Utilities, as they have lunch and swap wisecracks.

"Boy, did it rain or did it rain?"

"It was so bad I had to get up in the trees and swing to the truck."

The restaurant serves burgers and a variety of home-cooked platters, but the barbecue deserves first place on your list of choices. Open 11:00 A.M. to 8:30 P.M. every day but Sunday.

More commonly recommended when you ask about a place to eat, Boswells, at 406 Queen Street, a family-owned restaurant for nearly fifty years, specializes in fresh seafood, though you can also get standard entrees like steak and chicken. Beer, wine, and setups for brown baggers are available. Open Monday through Friday, 11:00 A.M. to 9:00 P.M.; Saturday, 5:00 to 9:30 P.M.; and Sunday, 11:00 A.M. to 2:30 P.M.

When you study North Carolina history, much of it seems to be about war campaigns, documents, and declarations. Two tour plantations in the area give you a more personal look at history on the day-to-day level.

Hope Plantation, about 20 miles west, in Windsor on State Highway 308 4 miles west of the highway bypass, re-creates rural domestic life in northeastern North Carolina during the colonial and federal periods. The plantation belonged to Governor David Stone, who also served in the state House of Commons and later as a United States senator. Stone owned more than 5,000 acres, planted mostly in wheat and corn. The plantation had all the mills, shops, and work areas necessary to be self-sufficient.

The two homes on the plantation, one dating from 1763, the other from about 1803, are examples of architecture that combines medieval English, Georgian, and neoclassical traits, reflecting the changing needs and knowledge of North Carolina colonists. Touring them, you see examples of how they might have been furnished, based on research about the plantation. The project continues to develop, so that eventually you'll be able to study a reconstruction of the kitchen on its original foundation, inspect relocated and restored outbuildings, and examine historically authentic vegetable and flower gardens. Moderate admission charged. Open March through December 23, Monday through Saturday, 10:00 A.M. to 4:00 P.M., and Sunday, 2:00 to 5:00 P.M. Closed Thanksgiving Day. For full information, write P.O. Box 610, Windsor, 27983, or call (919) 794-3140.

The second plantation deserves much wider attention. **Somerset Place,** a nineteenth-century coastal plantation near Creswell, belonged to Josiah Collins, a successful merchant who came to Edenton from England in 1774. He and other investors formed the Lake Company, which acquired more than 100,000 acres of land next to Lake Phelps. They dug (or, more accurately, had slaves dig) a 6-mile-long canal through an area known as the Great Alligator Dismal, to join the lake to the Scuppernong River and drain the swamps. When things were going well, gristmills and sawmills produced rice and lumber to ship down the canal in flatboats. But the flooding it takes to grow rice bred mosquitoes that made the slaves sick, so eventually the plantation grew corn and wheat instead.

Collins bought out his partners in 1816 and at his death passed the property on to his son. Later, Josiah Collins III took over. It seems Josiah Three, who went to Yale and graduated from law school in Connecticut, had a head for business. He turned Somerset Place into one of the state's largest plantations, working more than three hundred slaves by 1860. Most North Carolinians didn't own slaves; Collins was one of only four planters in the state with more than three hundred.

The great fascination in visiting Somerset Place lies in the uncommonly detailed records the Collins family kept, especially about the black people on the plantation. The records detailed not only births, deaths, and marriages but also jobs and skills. Thus today we know that the cook was Grace and that one slave, Luke Davis, had only one job, cleaning carpets. We know that two sons of Collins III were playing with two slave boys one winter when all four boys drowned in the canal.

Additional information comes from the accounts of Dr. John Kooner, a physician who used to stay at the plantation for several weeks at a time treating the slaves and the Collins family. He described an elaborate African dance that slaves Collins had imported directly from Africa apparently taught to the rest of the slave community. They performed it every year at Christmas, beginning at the great house, snaking to the overseer's house, and ending up at the slave quarters. Everyone on the plantation participated, either as a slave dancer or a spectator.

Archaeological exploration has turned up the remains of slave houses, a hospital and chapel, and the plantation's formal garden as well as the original brick boundary walls.

This kind of priceless information continues to come to light at Somerset Place, where personable and knowledgeable guides work hard to pass it on. You won't experience a routinized, canned tour here.

A dramatic sidebar to this story is that Dorothy Spruill Redford, a descendant of the Somerset slave families, published a book with Doubleday in 1988 entitled *Somerset Homecoming: Recovering a Lost Heritage.* In it she details the research it took to identify and find descendants of the Somerset families, describes contacting them, and tells about the huge, emotional reunion, or more accurately, first union, they held on the plantation. Redford includes much plantation history in her book as well.

Ultimately, the Civil War did in the plantation. The Collins family died elsewhere, and today the site is run by the state.

Somerset (919-797-4560) is open April 1 through October 31,

Monday through Saturday 9:00 A.M. to 5:00 P.M., Sunday 1:00 to 5:00 P.M.; November 1 through March 31, Tuesday through Saturday 10:00 A.M. to 4:00 P.M., Sunday 1:00 to 4:00 P.M. Closed Monday. These hours may vary; for details contact the site manager (P.O. Box 215, Creswell, 27928). Admission is free. At Creswell, the turn for the plantation is marked with a sign.

Off the Beaten Path in The Upper Piedmont

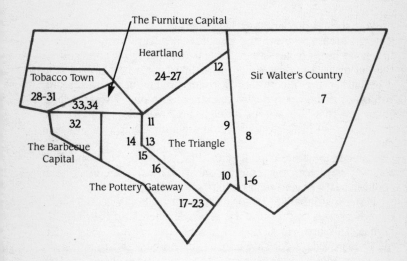

The Furniture Capital

Heartland

Tobacco Town

28-31

33,34

32

24-27

12

Sir Walter's Country

7

11

9

8

14 | 13   The Triangle

The Barbecue
Capital

15

16

10   1-6

The Pottery Gateway

17-23

1. Historic Oakwood
2. The Oakwood Inn
3. North Carolina Museum
   of History
4. North Carolina Museum
   of Natural Sciences
5. North Carolina Museum of Art
6. Jean-Claude's Cafe
7. La Grange Plantation Inn
8. Cedar Creek Gallery
9. Duke Homestead State Historic
   Site and Tobacco Museum
10. B. Everett Jordan Lake
11. Womancraft
12. Hillsborough
13. Fearrington Inn
14. North Carolina Zoological Park
15. Richard Petty Museum
16. Seagrove
17. Seagrove Pottery
18. Phil Morgan Pottery
19. J. B. Cole Pottery
20. Ben Owens Pottery
21. Westmoore Pottery
22. Dover Pottery
23. Jugtown
24. North Carolina A & T
    State University
25. Charlotte Hawkins Brown
    Memorial
26. Greensboro Historical Museum
27. Natural Science Center
28. R. J. Reynolds Tobacco U.S.A.
29. Old Salem
30. Museum of Early Southern
    Decorative Arts
31. Brookstown Inn
32. Lexington
33. Angela Peterson Doll and
    Miniature Museum
34. Springfield Museum
    of Old Domestic Art

The Upper Piedmont

Sir Walter's Country

You should probably get here soon if you want to enjoy the Raleigh area. Although the population hovers around several thousand more or less than 200,000, depending on your source, the entire area is developing or at least spreading out rapidly, especially in the direction of Durham. Driving along rural roads, you often come upon heavy equipment and newly cleared land. Tomorrow that land will be home to a new development. But the area is rich in history, culture, and amenities that it would be a shame to skip.

Raleigh, the state capital, named for Sir Walter Raleigh, offers a variety of historical sites, museums, and fine old architecture in addition to the government buildings downtown.

Plan on stopping at **Historic Oakwood,** at North Person Street between Jones and Boundary, if you're interested in Victorian homes. This historic district of more than four hundred homes, many restored, is considered one of the best examples of an unspoiled Victorian neighborhood in the country. Pick up a free walking-tour map that includes some history and descriptions of some of the buildings at the Capital Area Visitor Center, 301 North Blount Street. The center (919-733-3456) is open Monday through Friday, 8:00 A.M. to 5:00 P.M.; Saturday, 9:00 A.M. to 5:00 P.M.; and Sunday, 1:00 to 5:00 P.M. Closed Thanksgiving, December 24 and 25, and New Year's Day.

The Oakwood Inn, 411 North Bloodworth Street, in the district, offers guests a taste of high Victorian living, including a full breakfast, and also provides information about the district. The proprietor, Diana Newton, has been there a long time and can tell you about both history and current developments. Even the people at the visitors center recognize her knowledgeability and recommend her and the inn as a good source of information (919-832-9712).

As for the museums, two deserve your attention. The **North Carolina Museum of History** concentrates on exhibits, artifacts, and dioramas related to state history, transportation, and, of course, the revolutionary war and the Civil War. Guided tours are available Monday through Friday, but you need a reservation. Located at 109 East Jones Street, the museum (919-733-3894) is open Tuesday through Saturday, 9:00 A.M. to 5:00 P.M., and Sunday, 1:00 to 6:00 P.M. Closed major holidays. Admission free.

The **North Carolina Museum of Natural Sciences** is between Jones Street and Edenton at 102 North Salisbury Street (919-733-7450). Here you divide your attention between stuffed and skeletal remains of what once was and living specimens of what still is from across the state. In the whale hall, a 50-foot whale skeleton hung from the ceiling dominates the exhibits. The prize for live interest probably goes to a python. For twenty-five years, the python of note was 17-foot-long George, but he died with cancer when he was twenty-eight years old. Hapi, a mere baby at about six years and 15 feet, succeeds George. Hapi's acquisition interested North Carolinians enough to be written up in *Carolina Country* magazine. It seems she used to belong to Nannse and Richard I. Babcock, Jr., of Greenville and spent a lot of her time riding coiled up in the back window of the car, but as she grew she got too heavy to handle. The museum is pleased to have Hapi. Richard feels a little sad. "I'm going to miss him. He's been my buddy for a long time," Richard told the magazine, which is a little confusing, given that "he" is definitely a she. But maybe the Babcocks felt shy about looking. Museum hours are the same as those at the museum of history. Admission is free.

Also, allow time for the **North Carolina Museum of Art** at 2110 Blue Ridge Avenue (take the Wade Avenue exit off Interstate 40). The building, designed by the architect Edward Durrell Stone, who designed the John F. Kennedy Center in Washington D. C. and the original Museum of Modern Art in New York, is important; so are the eight major collections. Arranged in chronological order, they cover five hundred years of western art, displaying work by artists from Botticelli to Monet to Andrew Wyeth. You'll also find exhibits of Jewish ceremonial art, Greek and Roman sculpture, and Japanese antique kimonos. Tours are available at 1:30 P.M. A cafe and gift shop operate during museum hours. The museum (919-733-7450) is open Tuesday through Saturday, 10:00 A.M. to 5:00 P.M., and Sunday, noon to 5:00 P.M. Closed Monday. Admission free.

Attending to your dinner, a restaurant in the area really appeals to the kinds of people who read a book like this. **Jean-Claude's Cafe** serves country French food in a small, unassuming dining room, mostly to local folks who believe they're keeping the place a secret. The restaurant is in North Ridge Shopping Center, unlikely as that sounds for such a find. (Take the Old Wake Forest Road exit from the beltline and go north 3 miles on what becomes Falls of Neuse Avenue.) The menu includes a country pâté that could be a meal in itself; soup du jour specialties, such as cream of pumpkin; and entrees like French sauerkraut with pork and mixed sausages, to make your mouth water and bust your belt, at surprisingly moderate prices. The unquestioned favorite, however, is the salmon in puff pastry. You can order nice wines and imported beers here, too. Open Monday through Saturday, 11:00 A.M. to 2:00 P.M. and 5:30 P.M. to 9:00 P.M. Closed Sunday and holidays (919-872-6224).

People who enjoy Jean-Claude's also like the Irregardless Cafe, at 901 West Morgan Street. When they describe it, people tend to call it the "vegetarian restaurant," but it does serve chicken and fish as well as the vegetarian entrees. Don't be fooled by the sprouts in the salads. These aren't old hippies or young health food nuts; they're folks who've figured out how to get the best flavor out of fresh ingredients with the least amount of doctoring. To dispel the notion that you're doing something that's good for you, you can order anything you like from the full bar. The homemade desserts will keep you on the sinful side too. Open for lunch Monday through Friday, 11:30 A.M to 2:15 P.M.; dinner Monday through Thursday, 5:00 to 9:30 P.M., Friday and Saturday to 10:00 P.M.

If you like gardens and plants and farmers, you'll want to add two more stops to your itinerary—the Raleigh Farmers Market and the North Carolina State University Arboretum. The Farmers Market, 1301 Hodges Street, in the warehouse section of town, draws crowds of locals with local fresh produce sold by truck farmers in the area. Even if you're traveling and don't want to haul a lot of carrots across the state, it's fun to wander around watching the people and sampling the wares. Depending on your taste in fresh fruits and vegetables, it might be a little more fun to visit here during spring strawberry season or summer peach time than, say, for fall turnips or winter squash, but the market is open year-round, 5:00 A.M. to 6:00 P.M., every day but Sunday. The arboretum, on Beryl Street (take the Hillsborough Street exit off the beltline) grows thousands of plants from around the world. In addition to special interest areas, such as the silver and white garden and a Japanese garden, a long perennial garden shows what it's possible to grow outside in North Carolina every month of the year. Open daily from 8:00 A.M. to 5:00 P.M. Admission free (919-737-3132).

For a nice break from the city, head north, either on Highway 1 or on Highway 401 and Highway 39, to Henderson, not far from the Virginia border, to spend the night at **La Grange Plantation Inn** (919-438-2421). Dick and Jean Cornell are the proprietors and innkeepers and are outstandingly hospitable people. In 1985 the Cornells bought the historical house, built in 1770, restored it, added a new building for kitchen and dining room, put in a swimming pool and an estatelike lawn, designed gardens, and cleaned up a picturesque old family cemetery on the property. Then they grabbed a couple quick breaths and launched into the bed and breakfast business. The inn has five guest rooms, all with private bath, and is furnished English country style (Jean is English), with American and English antiques and reproductions comfortably arranged throughout. The parlor has a fireplace but no television; bedrooms have comfortable chairs with reading lamps; books fill shelves everywhere. The rural setting, lawn, fields, and woods that end at the edge of Lake Kerr slow you down and relax you almost instantly. One frequent guest says, "It's like an oasis. It feels like coming home." You can hike, watch birds, fish, or snooze. If your energy zooms, the Cornells can arrange for you to golf or play tennis at their country club nearby.

If you like good food, maybe you should have going-home clothes a size bigger. Jean's breakfasts, included in the rates, are creative and delicious and include several different breads and muffins. Sometimes she makes lemon curd, a British treat, to go with them. Guests known for their austerity have been caught having thirds.

While you're in the area, treat yourself to the **Cedar Creek Gallery,** a workplace and sales outlet for top quality craftspeople. Their brochure says, "Expect to be overwhelmed," and that's not hype. The gallery displays meander through many rooms. Much of the work is pottery, but you'll also find fine glass, handmade stereopticans, stringed instruments, jewelry, and toys that are too splendid to put into the hands of kids. The quality is so outstanding that people tend to walk along talking in hushed tones, though that's not at all the demeanor of the artisans themselves. From Henderson, go south on Interstate 85, take the second Butner exit (186), turn left on Highway 15 north, turn right at the first crossroads, and left on Fleming Road to the gallery. Open daily, 10:00 A.M. to 6:00 P.M. (919-528-1041).

As a final indulgence in this area, stop at Bob's Bar-B-Que, on Highway 56 between Creedmore and Interstate 85. Not only can you get good North Carolina barbecue here, but you can also dig into a serving of bunter stew, made with beef, pork, limas, and potatoes. Might as well just leave on those going-home clothes. The traditional beverage is iced tea, sweet or unsweetened, served in plastic cups with the name of the restaurant on the side. Open Monday through Saturday, 10:00 A.M. to 8:15 P.M. (919-528-2081).

The Triangle

In a sense, Durham is closer to Raleigh than it used to be. With both communities expanding laterally, it's not hard as you drive between the two places to imagine that they'll soon run together. Durham is a tobacco town; the major university, Duke University, was endowed by and named for the Duke family, which made Durham a tobacco center.

Although tobacco is not as important in the area as it once was, criticizing smokers is not a good way to make friends here. The Duke family pioneered in marketing cigarettes in America. You can understand something of the mystique and importance of tobacco by visiting the **Duke Homestead State Historic Site and Tobacco Museum,** established on the Duke family farm. Take the Guess Road exit off Interstate 85 to 2828 Duke Home-stead Road. Depending on when you're here, you'll see tobacco being planted, cultivated, harvested, or prepared for market and have the opportunity to participate in part of the processing.

On the property, the old family house, two tobacco factories, a curing barn, and a packhouse show you how it used to be. In the visitor center, tobacco-related exhibits include advertising, signs, machinery, and an old cigar store Indian. A twenty-minute film, "Carolina Bright" (the local name for brightleaf tobacco) describes the history and importance of tobacco in the state in a more positive light than most of what you see and hear today. Admission is free. Open Tuesday through Saturday, 9:00 A.M. to 5:00 P.M., and Sunday, 1:00 to 5:00 P.M. Closed Monday, Christmas

Day, and Thanksgiving. Hours change, so it's a good idea to call ahead (919-477-5498).

A convenient but away-from-town place to stay is the Arrowhead Inn Bed and Breakfast, about 7 miles north of Interstate 85 on Highway 501 at 106 Mason Road, Durham, 27712. The manor house was built shortly before the Revolution. Jerry and Barbara Ryan renovated it and, in turning it into a bed and breakfast, earned an award from the Durham Historic Preservation Society for adaptive reuse in 1987. That's interesting when you consider the need in the area to find new uses for tobacco land and, eventually, some of the edifices devoted to processing and selling tobacco. Rates here include a full country breakfast with fruit, meat, eggs, and homemade breads. The Ryans keep a guidebook of local restaurants to help you find the kind of place that appeals to you for dinner (919-777-8430).

Whether for dinner or lunch, if you like to taste local beers, don't miss the Weeping Radish microbrewery and restaurant, sister to the Weeping Radish in Manteo. The menu features German specialties such as sauerbraten and Wiener schnitzel, and the brewery produces beer from an old German recipe. The restaurant is at 115 North Duke Street (919-682-2337). Open Monday through Saturday, 11:30 to 2:00 P.M. and 5:30 to 10:00 P.M.

While you're in the Triangle, take a picnic to the **B. Everett Jordan Lake,** a 47,000-acre lake created by the United States Army Corps of Engineers for flood control. All water recreation is available at some part of the lake—boating, swimming, fishing, as well as hiking and camping. As you drive around in the area, you'll probably notice several different roads, all marked with signs, leading into access areas. One is Highway 64 at Highway 51, which leads to several recreation areas. Another is off Highway 64 going north on Highway 15/501, a point southwest of Durham, which takes you from Pittsboro, through Bynum and into Chapel Hill, home of the University of North Carolina at Chapel Hill. Chapel Hill and Durham are so close together that residents frequently live in one community and work in the other. The area south of Chapel Hill is still fairly rural and is a popular living area for university people with an itch to rusticate.

Chapel Hill, almost the geographical center of North Carolina, is recognizably a college town, the kind where the campus and the town meet at a wall running along the campus green, where students sit on the wall to see and be seen, and where the businesses across the street are mostly campus oriented. Visitors actually tour the campus, less because of its history than because it is so Norman Rockwellish, sort of an artist's conceptualization of a campus, with trees and grass and historic buildings—even some ivy here and there.

In the college atmosphere, **Womancraft,** a retail gallery of area artisans, seems to be just what you'd expect. Forty craftswomen sell handmade quilts, weavings, jewelry, toys, and pottery in the cooperative. They take pains to offer seasonally appropriate items for Christmas and other special times. The shop (919-929-8362) is at 412 West Franklin Street (Highway 15/501), west of Highway 86 heading toward Carrboro. Open Monday through Saturday, 10:00 A.M. to 5:30 P.M.

Make a quick 12-mile side trip north on Highway 86 to **Hillsborough,** where a lot of history is condensed in a small area. Hillsborough was a capital of colonial and revolutionary North Carolina and a center of politics. During the Revolution, troops of Cornwallis grouped for deployment here. The state convention to ratify the federal Constitution met here in 1788; in 1865 the Confederate general who signed the surrender of the Civil War headquartered here. Colonial, antebellum, and Victorian architecture mingle comfortably along the streets. The Hillsborough Historical Society likes to say that the town is a living, not a reconstructed, community.

At the Orange County Historical Museum or the Town Hall you can pick up an annotated map for a walking tour. For further information from the historical society, phone (919) 732-8648 mornings.

Food is available at the Regulator Cafe, 108 South Churchton Street (919-732-5600), lodging and southern cooking at Colonial Inn, 153 West King Street (919-732-1120).

South of Chapel Hill on Highway 15/501, shortly after you pass the access roads to the lake between Bynum and Pittsboro, two more women practice their craft in a ramshackle-looking building beside the road. Neolia and Celia Cole make pottery in the North Carolina production tradition, specializing in sponge ware, a soft brownish glaze called "butterware," and a shocking red glaze. The pots at Cole's Pottery, 3410 Hawkins Avenue, Sanford, are not the sleek stylish pieces of studio potters, but the made-for-use mugs, bowls, pitchers, and teapots of the kind that served local people for daily use in earlier days. The sisters also make a variety of miniature tea sets and vases. They sign each piece with a comment like, "Love, Neolia Cole," and "Let me go home with you." Their stock, like that of most North Carolina potters, fluctuates with demand. Sometimes they can hardly keep up, and the shelves will be sparsely filled; other times pots crowd every available inch. Nobody gets upset if you stop in, look around, and leave without having bought anything. Open Monday through Friday, 8:00 A.M. to 5:30 P.M., and Saturday, 8:30 A.M. to 3:30 P.M. (919-776-9558).

In Pittsboro you need to see **Fearrington Inn** even if you can't afford to stay there. And many of us cannot! The inn is part of Fearrington Village, a remarkably tasteful planned community settled into the rural countryside, side by side with pastures and productive fields. The creators, J. B. and Jenny Fitch, mean to preserve the old Fearrington farm and its buildings, adding a new country village to the acreage. One of the first things you notice is funny-looking cows in the fields. They're belted Galloway cows, from Scotland. They look as though their middles had been wrapped in Ace bandages about 2 feet wide. They're a passion of J. B.'s.

When you stay at the inn or eat at Fearrington House, a few steps away, you become part of the village. The restaurant is in the old homestead. The inn is newly built to match the homestead and decorated in country English style with chintz and live plants and English pine antiques. Wide windows let in sunlight everywhere. The wood for the beautiful pale floors was imported from England.

If you like the inn's accessories, you'll like Jenny Fitch's gift shop, the Southern Country Garden Shop. The complex also includes Pringle Pottery, a fine studio potter, and a new bookstore about which sales representatives rave. In the general store, you can pick up a gourmet lunch of pasta or unusual sandwiches in the Market Cafe. For a full dinner, the award-winning Fearrington House specializes in traditional southern foods prepared in unusual new ways: smoked quail with veal forcemeat, boneless loin of lamb with a bourbon, molasses, and butter sauce, fried sweet potatoes. Beer and wine are available. The restaurant is open Tuesday through Saturday, 6:30 A.M. to 9:00 P.M., and Sunday, 11:00 A.M. to 2:00 P.M. The phone number for both the restaurant and inn is (919) 542-2121.

From Pittsboro it's an easy drive of no more than 40 miles west on Highway 64, mostly through rural countryside, to

Asheboro. Going in every direction from Asheboro, you have wonderful possibilities.

The Pottery Gateway

Although the area bustles with activity, don't look for anything special in the way of food or lodging. Steakhouses and a few motels are about all you'll find, but these are pleasant and entirely acceptable when you just need a meal and a night's sleep, not an experience.

For an *experience*, go to the south side of Asheboro on Highway 220, where signs and arrows direct you to the **North Carolina Zoological Park.** The zoo (919-879-5606) is big, on more than a thousand acres, though not all are being used yet. It's famous, and it's certainly not far off a beaten path. Go anyway. It got to be big and famous because they're doing such a good job with the concept of keeping the animals in natural environments without bars. Sometimes a natural gulf separates the people from the animals, sometimes a clear barrier. For instance, the aviary, under a glass dome, houses hundreds of exotic birds in with thousands of tropical plants. In other sections you can watch elephants, herds of antelope, and even crocodiles, all apparently blissfully unaware of an audience or confinement. Seeing everything involves walking a couple miles or more, but for a modest fee you can ride in a tram that follows the same route as the footpaths. Modest admission fee. Open Monday through Friday, 9:00 A.M. to 5:00 P.M., and Saturday and Sunday, 10:00 A.M. to 6:00 P.M.

From the natural to something near the ultimate in machinery, the **Richard Petty Museum** displays race cars, trophies, and films of famous races on the grounds of Petty's garages. Most of the awards belong to Richard, but some belong to Lee Petty, his father. Sometimes the garages are open for tours. Showcases commemorate Petty's two hundredth win and his one thousandth start. If you know about NASCAR racing fans, the intense partying that goes along with any race day for some of them, and have seen the huge banners advertising Goody's Headache Powders that go up at convenience stores on big race weekends, you may find humor in the Goody's Mini-Theater and Photos. Among the displays are a Chrysler Hemi engine and several race cars, all number 43. (Every car Richard Petty drives is number 43.)

Racing is so important in North Carolina that the results of all races in which local drivers participate are broadcast on local television sports news. Petty is a much-loved North Carolina hero. It would be a mistake, however, to suppose this is a uniquely North Carolina phenomenon. Among Petty's artifacts are letters of congratulations from presidents Ford, Reagan, and Bush.

Petty's winning days at the races seem to have ended, but his reputation as the king of racing remains intact. Even if you neither know that Petty is the king of racing nor care a fig for the sport, you might find spending some time among people who do a fascinating cultural experience. Signs off Highway 220 near the zoo signs south of Asheboro at the Level Cross exit direct you to the museum. Modest admission fee; children under twelve free. Open Monday through Saturday, 10:00 A.M. to 4:00 P.M. (919-495-1143).

You could spend all day at the zoo; the Richard Petty Museum needs only an hour or so; the next attraction, **Seagrove,** and the potteries could take a week. When you drive into pottery country, you'll find almost nothing in the way of food, so eat hearty in the morning before you leave, or pack a picnic. Before you start, accept the fact that it's physically impossible to stop at every pottery in one day. It was impossible a few years ago when they numbered in the thirties; now that there are more than fifty, your only alternatives are to choose your stops selectively or to plan several trips.

Originally this part of the country attracted production potters who made the storage jugs, pitchers, crocks, and bean pots farmers used every day because both the heavy red clay for potting and the timber stands for fueling the kilns were right here. No doubt local moonshine was one of the products that got stored in the jugs. A rich culture developed around potting, complete with family traditions in design and glazing. Some, such as Ben Owens, earned reputations for being excellent turners.

As other materials came along for making utensils to cook and store food, the potters turned more to producing items for tourists. But the actual potting stayed basically the same. Over three and four generations, feuds and disagreements came up, and sometimes a member of a famous potting family, such as Owens, would splinter off to start an independent pottery.

The old families continue making the same kinds of pottery today. Tourists and gift shop owners buy it up faster than the

North Carolina Potters

wheels at Cole and Jugtown and Owens can turn.

Newcomers fill out the scene with more artistic studio pottery, which is usually more elaborately shaped, decorated, and glazed. These pieces take longer to make.

Some of the new potters are local young people who have studied in the well-respected program at the Troy Technical College nearby. Others, transplants from elsewhere, have been attracted by the concentration of potters that attracts customers and ensures support.

Many of the materials these days are shipped in from elsewhere rather than dug from local ground, and some kilns are fired by oil, gas, or electricity rather than wood. But the atmosphere is still that of a unique culture engrossed in a hands-on kind of work.

Some people say the old-timers don't think much of the new

crowd because they're too fancy. Some people say the newcomers look down on the "production mentality" of the old families. Those attitudes may exist, but what you'll usually hear is encouragement from the long-established potters for the new ones, and deep respect and admiration from the newer people for the speed and accuracy with which a good production potter can turn. As one young man said, "I've been futzing with this lid for two hours now. Those guys would've finished a dozen pots in that time."

Wherever you stop, talk to the people. They're used to it, they like it, and it's an integral part of the experience. As you do, you can't help notice the arthritic hands of some of the old potters. As a younger artisan explained it, "My pots will never be quite as good as theirs, because you need to keep wetting the clay with *cold* water for the very best results, and I use warm water. I've seen what twenty and thirty years of cold water and clay does to your hands. I'm afraid I'm not quite that dedicated."

To get into the heart of the pottery district, start at **Seagrove Pottery,** just north of Seagrove on Highway 220. The unpretentious, rambling, low, frame building on the left is easy to miss. If you do, turn around and go back. Seagrove Pottery is a must-see place, one of the most famous of the early potteries, where today you still might easily walk in and see a child making his first experiments in clay with the encouragement from his grandmother. Seagrove pottery is known especially for its traditional muted green and rusty-colored glazes. Once you've seen the pottery, you'll recognize it anywhere. Displays of very early Seagrove pieces, not for sale, give you a sense of how the craft has developed and also how it has stayed the same. Here, as at any of the potteries, you can pick up a hand-drawn map of the area, with all the potteries listed and located. The largest concentration of potteries begins on Highway 705, off Highway 220. The state road numbers are clearly marked, so it is easy to follow the map through the countryside, traveling from one pottery to another. No two are alike, nor are their wares. Part of the fun is in the discovery and surprise; you don't need full information ahead of time about each place, but following are a few guaranteed to be special. They are all marked on the free maps available at every pottery.

Phil Morgan Pottery (919-873-7304) features Phil's elegant crystalline glazes on porcelain and his wife's more traditional earthenware, much of it in pleasing muted rose and blue tones decorated with flowers. These people love to talk and can give you what seems like a complete course in the intricacies of crystalline glazing.

J. B. Cole Pottery (919-873-7171) has a huge expanse of tables and shelves in the requisite old frame building. If you can get here in early spring, March or earlier, after they've had time to stock up from the Christmas rush, the shelves and tables are laden with earthenware dinner plates, sandwich plates, bowls, pitchers, and other items in a variety of colorful glazes. A glossy deep blue and a pebbly white are probably most commonly associated with Cole's. The people here are always busy, but friendly and great talkers even as they work. There's a public bathroom here, which becomes more important than you'd guess driving through the countryside.

Ben Owens Pottery (919-464-2261) displays the work of Ben Owens III, who was recognized as a boy for having superior talent, on a par with that of his grandfather. Young Ben works as an artist, producing shapes and designs inspired by Egyptian and Japanese work. His pots are on display in museums around the country, and he is teaching pottery classes at Pfeiffer College while he is enrolled there as a student. The display rooms usually aren't heavily stocked, but you do find an interesting variety, presided over by a proud papa who can explain Ben's work in detail.

At **Westmoore Pottery** (919-464-3700), open only since 1977, Mary and David Farrell make reproductions of the earthenware and salt-glazed stoneware typical of the eighteenth and early nineteenth centuries. They also make stunning reproductions of Moravian pottery as well as create new designs in the old traditions.

Mary can throw a pot or apply a Moravian-design slip trail without a flaw and chat with customers at the same time. The couple and the pottery have recently received national attention in more than one country-oriented magazine for their work and the unique new home they built behind their new pottery. Their work is especially popular with people involved in authentic historic restoration and representation.

Milly McCanless of **Dover Pottery** (919-464-3586), is one of the new potters too. Initially, she got into it because she had a dollhouse and wanted to learn to throw miniature pots for her miniature dining table. In the process she discovered that she was also good with big pots. She saw that while there wasn't much market for miniatures, she could sell as much full-sized pottery as she could produce. She's especially known for pieces beautifully decorated in painted floral and bird designs. "It's functional art. I love the idea," she says. If you like to laugh, stop here. Milly is fun.

Jugtown (919-464-3266) operates somewhat more commercially than the other potteries, including handwoven rugs and placemats, handmade toys, and other North Carolina folk crafts in its retail stock. The Jugtown stoneware is uniform enough in appearance to look nice beside the more regular, mass-produced commercial dinnerware and seems practically indestructible. Most of the pieces reflect traditional local styles and glazes. There is a bathroom here too.

The hours of the various potters may vary by a half hour or so in opening and closing, but most are open from 8:30 A.M. to 4:30 P.M., Monday through Saturday. All are closed Sunday. The best time to go is Friday afternoon, when most of the kilns are opened to bring out the new pots. Saturday morning is a good time too, but by afternoon the wares will already be thinning out. It's almost a waste of time to go around Christmas or in late summer. The shoppers then simply buy faster than the potters can pot.

Although some early glazes contained lead, today's are lead-free and safe for table use. If you have any concerns about lead, ask in the pottery.

Heartland

Another possible trip from Asheboro is the short hop up Highway 220 to Greensboro, a pleasant city with a historic downtown and lots of surprises. There's some revolutionary war history here, in a strange sort of way. Cornwallis won a battle against General Nathan Greene's American troops, but in the process lost so many men that he ultimately had to surrender at Yorktown. The Guilford Courthouse National Military Park, 6 miles north of Greensboro on Highway 220, commemorates the loss and the win with exhibits on the battlefield and displays and films in the visitors center (919-288-1776). The center is open daily, 8:30 A.M. to 5:00 P.M. Admission free.

Drawing on more recent events, Greensboro holds special significance for blacks. In 1960 black students from **North Carolina A & T State University** (originally the Agricultural and Mechanical College for the Colored Race) began the first sit-ins at Woolworth's segregated lunch counter. A & T is Jesse Jackson's alma mater, and he still comes to town from time to time.

On the campus of North Carolina A & T State University the Mattye Reed African Heritage Center displays African masks, paintings, black history books, and art objects. Open Monday through Friday. Call for current hours (919-334-7874). Admission free.

Less than 10 miles east of Greensboro, the **Charlotte Hawkins Brown Memorial,** a still-developing state historic site, honors Dr. Brown's fifty years as head of another school for blacks, Palmer Memorial Institute. The buildings are gradually being restored, and plans are to make the memorial a center for contributions of North Carolina blacks, including a research center with collection and computer facilities devoted to North Carolina black history. Open Tuesday through Saturday, 10:00 A.M. to 4:00 P.M., April through October (919-449-6515). Admission free. For further information on development of the site, write Historic Sites Section, 109 East Jones Street, Raleigh, 27611.

Local history from the time of the early Indians to date shapes the displays at the **Greensboro Historical Museum,** 130 Summit Avenue, in what used to be the First Presbyterian Church. In a re-creation of nineteenth-century Greensboro, the museum shows a general store, the drugstore where William Sydney Porter (O. Henry) once worked, a post office, a law office, a firehouse, a cobbler's, and a blacksmith's.

Other exhibits include room settings from historical homes, an exhibit of household items and clothing of Dolley Madison (a Greensboro native before she became first lady), and a collection of antique automobiles. Open Tuesday through Saturday, 10:00 A.M. to 5:00 P.M., and Sunday, 2:00 to 5:00 P.M. (919-373-2043). Admission free.

One stop that could be a treat for those who love dollhouses and miniatures is Portrait House, the photography studio of Vivian Robinson. In addition to exhibits of her photography and paintings by her husband, Stan, Vivian displays a fully landscaped Edwardian estate that she created in the inch-to-the-foot scale. A formal wedding party fills the lawn around the gazebo and fountain. An overweight cook and a sour-faced butler that she sculpted and dressed preside over the elegant wedding buffet. Altogether, Vivian dressed twenty-two dolls in Edwardian costumes. The dogwoods and redbuds are in full bloom; goldfish swim in the pond. Vivian ingeniously created realistic-looking trees and shrubs and even carved a copy of a Lutyens bench by hand. And just to show that she had the Victorians in perspective, she settled Mary Poppins, umbrella, suitcase, and all, atop the chimney. Vivian says that she would sell the project, so you'd better call ahead to be sure it's still there if you'd like to see it, but you probably won't be disappointed, because she has put a supercalafragilistic price on it (919–272–4382).

If you're traveling with kids (or even if you're not, come to think of it), don't miss the **Natural Science Center,** 4301 Lawndale Drive (919–288–3769), where you can easily spend a day immersing yourself in the sights and sounds of everything from dinosaurs to star systems. This is a "participation museum," where you don't have to tell the kids to look, not touch. For instance, you can put your hand into a real dinosaur footprint, pet and feed animals in the zoo, observe sunspots in the live solar observatory, and turn your imagination loose in the planetarium. The transparent anatomical mannequin, which you might want to save until after lunch, lets you study what goes on inside the skin of the human body. The museum is open Monday through Saturday, 9:00 A.M. to 5:00 P.M., and Sunday, 1:00 to 5:00 P.M. Admission free. The zoo is open Monday through Saturday, 10:00 A.M. to 4:30 P.M., and Sunday, 1:00 to 4:30 P.M. Nominal admission charged.

When you've had enough of history, science, and culture and need revitalizing, the 230 House Tea Room, at 230 North Spring Street (919–333–2834), is simply perfect. This tea room actually serves tea, real tea, thirteen different kinds, made without tea bags in a real teapot. Miriam Emerson, who owns the tea room, feels passionately on the subject of tea and loves to tell you all you want to know about it as you're drinking it. She's modeled her place on the classic English tea room, where people really do stop for tea, as opposed to the American department store "tea room" where you tend to grab a Coke and a chicken salad sandwich. But, weary sightseers do not live by tea alone, so by reservation you can also have lunch. The salads and sandwiches that make up the menu are always made to order from fresh ingredients, which gives you a little time to enjoy your first cup of tea before you eat. The tea room is open Monday through Friday for lunch from 11:30 A.M. to 6:00 P.M. and for afternoon tea from 2:30 to 6:00 P.M. Brunch is served on Saturday from 10:00 A.M. to 3:00 P.M. and on Sunday from 11:30 A.M. to 3:00 P.M.

For a full meal, try the Atrium, 4721 Lawndale Drive (919–282–7799), a family-owned restaurant that is always busy with local trade without ever needing to advertise. The menu features a good range from the exotic to standard American entrees. You'll find calamari and kabobs, but also steaks and pasta. Dress is relatively casual. As one local resident explains, "You wouldn't wear jeans, but you wouldn't wear a suit and tie, either. It's the Izod sweater crowd. You're bound to see at least two pairs of lime green pants when you go." The restaurant has a full liquor license. Open Monday through Saturday for dinner from 5:00 to 10:00 P.M. Closed Sunday.

Drop your weary head on a pillow at the Greenwich—a small, older, European-style hotel downtown—or at the Greenwood Bed and Breakfast, in one of Greenboro's first suburban areas, about 10 blocks from the business district. The Greenwich, 111 West Washington Street (919-272-3474), has had what the cliche makers would call "a checkered past." It was built to be corporate headquarters for a textile company in the 1800s, then was used as a post office, and later was turned into a hospital during World War II. In the twenty years before it was rescued and renovated, it had been either a house of ill repute (the ultimate game of post office) or a flophouse, depending on whose story you believe. A little of both may have been true. Now the lobby is a pretty little area of brass and crystal chandeliers and eighteenth-century reproductions and art. The rooms are tasteful and comfortable, with small refrigerators to cool your traveling comestibles.

The Greenwood (919-274-6350), a stick-style home built in the early 1900s, has also been renovated. Old oaks and magnolias and the neighborhood park surround the home with greenery and shield the backyard swimming pool from the curious. Some of the five rooms share baths unless you request otherwise. The hostess, Jo Anne Green, serves a continental breakfast with fruit and homemade breads, which is included in the rates.

Tobacco Town

From Greensboro, you're looking at a drive of only about 20 miles west on Interstate 40 to Winston-Salem, the tobacco town. It would be hard to overstate the influence of the R. J. Reynolds Tobacco Company. While Richard Joshua Reynolds was directing a rapidly growing business and hiring increasing thousands of people in the tobacco factories, his wife set about a long series of community improvement activities for the benefit of those same families. With Reynolds money and Moravian artistic influence, the area developed into a cultural center that still ranks high in the country today.

Perhaps the most audacious Reynolds act in later years was the lock-stock-and-barrel move of Wake Forest University from Wade County to Winston-Salem in 1950. President Truman came to wield the shovel in the ground-breaking ceremony.

To learn more about the tobacco industry and the Reynolds influence in it, stop at the **R. J. Reynolds Tobacco U.S.A.** plant 3 miles north of Greensboro on Highway 52 for a guided tour of the plant that produces 450 *million* cigarettes a day, and a stop in the museum that depicts the development of the industry. Notice the heavy sweet smell of tobacco that permeates the air. Line workers who are close to the actual tobacco products will tell you that the smell gets into their clothes and remains so strong that after work at home they may shuck their work clothes at the doorway to keep the smell out of the house.

As background on the R.J.R. dynasty, you should read the recent book by Patrick Reynolds (who has come out strongly against using tobacco) and Tom Shachtman, *The Gilded Leaf: Triumph, Tragedy, and Tobacco—Three Generations of the R. J. Reynolds Family and Fortune.* Larry Hagman wrote that it made Dallas look "like a bowl of warm milk toast." Be careful about trying to discuss the book while you're here, though. Criticizing tobacco in a community built upon it rouses the ire of some residents. So does speaking ill of the First Tobacco Family.

About half a century ago, the town was shocked when Zachary Smith Reynolds, usually called Smith, son of R. J. and Katharine, was shot through the head during a boozy party at the family home, less than a year after his marriage to the torch singer Libby Holman. Apparently Smith Reynolds caught Libby flirting (or more) with a friend, fighting erupted, and Smith either shot himself or was killed by Libby. Newspapers suppressed much of the story at the time, and even today, polite society doesn't talk about it, though that hasn't stopped brazen authors from writing about it. An interesting source, should you decide to pursue the subject further, is the biography entitled *Libby Holman: Body and Soul,* by H. D. Perry.

After studying the impact of Reynolds and tobacco, turn your attention to the Moravians. Moravians came from Pennsylvania to settle the area in 1753. They built Salem as a totally planned, church-governed community in 1766. Winston wasn't founded until

1849. In Salem, arts and crafts flourished; in Winston, it was tobacco and textiles. By the early 1900s, the two towns had grown together and consolidated. It would be hard to say whether tobacco or the Moravians left the greater mark on the area, nor is it really pertinent; in the early days tobacco wasn't a dirty word, and nobody saw anything wrong with a strong relationship between church and chew.

If you see only one attraction here, it certainly should be **Old Salem,** a Moravian town restored so carefully that when you walk the streets and go into the buildings you feel as though you've entered Rod Serling's time warp. To give you an idea of the pains staff people take with getting it right, people responsible for demonstrations of cooking and household activities take turns preparing research papers and consulting old diaries, journals, and letters to discover exactly how the households might have run. Unlike traditional historians who mainly study battles, politics, and industrial development, these re-creators also try to piece together the elements of day-to-day life. This isn't the only historic site where such activities are going on, but it's hard to imagine one where they're being treated any more earnestly or where the subject matter is any more fascinating. This attention to detail extends even to the food cooked from old Moravian recipes. The original recipe used fresh ginger root, but gingerbread recipes in later years have shifted to powdered ginger because it's easier to find and keep. The Old Salem recipe still specifies fresh, grated ginger.

Costumed guides in the old kitchen cook in the huge fireplace and iron with flatirons heated there, all the while sweating genuine sweat—a fascinating reminder in this age of air conditioning that just getting from one day to the next took a lot of energy. Among the demonstrations offered in Old Salem are music from an organ built in 1797, potting, baking, and spinning.

Not all the buildings in the historic district are restored as tour buildings. Some are private homes. The presence of automobiles and real people living real lives doesn't seem to detract from the atmosphere; indeed it simply makes it feel more alive. Whatever tours you take, start at the visitors center (919-721-7300). Open Monday through Saturday, 10:30 A.M. to 4:30 P.M., and Sunday, 1:30 to 4:30 P.M. Moderate to high admission fees, depending on how many features you wish to tour.

Having toured Old Salem, you'll need to eat at the Old Salem

Tavern Dining Rooms at 736 South Main Street in the district (919-748-8585). Continuing the sense of reenactment, costumed staff serve Moravian-style cooking by candlelight. Specialties include game and gingerbread from the old recipes. For the faint of palate, standard beef and chop entrees are also available. All spirits served. Open Monday through Friday from 11:30 A.M. to 2:00 P.M. for lunch; dinner served Monday through Thursday, 5:30 to 9:00 P.M., and Friday and Saturday, 5:30 to 9:30 P.M.

Old Salem

Also in Old Salem, the **Museum of Early Southern Decorative Arts** (919-722-6148) gives you a close look at the results of extensive research into the regional decorative arts of the early south. The exhibits include furniture, paintings, textiles, ceramics, silver, and other metalwares. You can't just wander in here. Guides take you through the building in small groups. You may buy tickets at the Old Salem Visitors Center. Museum hours are Monday through Saturday, 10:30 A.M. to 4:30 P.M., and Sunday, 1:30 to 4:30 P.M.

An appropriate end to a day in this historic, manufacturing, and artistic town is a night's lodging at **Brookstown Inn,** a restored 1837 textile mill (919-725-1120). The history of the inn matches that of the city for interest. Moravians opened the Salem Cotton Manufacturing Company and later sold it, and the buildings were subsequently used as a flour mill and then as a moving-company storage house. The conversion to an inn created large guest rooms with odd nooks and crannies and high ceilings, an upstairs wall covered with the graffiti (protected by an acrylic plastic sheet) of the young factory girls who boarded there, and a boiler room with catwalk that now serves as a restaurant in which one of the old boiler faces is a focal point. The decor is early American, with many handmade quilts and country accents. Rates include wine and cheese in the parlor and continental breakfast in the dining room.

As you leave the area, to move swiftly back into the twentieth century you might stop at the Nature Science Center, 7 1/2 miles north of the intersection of Interstate 40 on Highway 52 on Museum Drive off the Hanes Mill Road exit. The participatory exhibits cover natural science and physical science and technology. One of the most poignant exhibits is the space shuttle display showing the *Challenger,* made possible by money schoolchildren in North Carolina raised to memorialize Christa McAuliffe. In related exhibits, a three-dimensional solar system display puts you in the middle of the planets, and a model of the moon shows the landing sites of Apollo. Modest admission fee. The museum (919-767-6730) is open Monday through Saturday, 10:00 A.M. to 5:00 P.M., and Sunday, 1:00 to 5:00 P.M.

The Barbecue Capital

Also on Highway 52, about 20 miles south, the town of **Lexington** is a must stop for barbecue freaks. More than a dozen different restaurants in this little town serve pork barbecue (if it's made with anything else it isn't really barbecue!) "Lexington style," which means a tomato-vinegar sauce. Elsewhere in the state, the sauce, which is always added later rather than simmered with the pork, contains only hot pepper and vinegar. And it never, never contains mustard. That's South Carolina barbecue. Sometimes you'll see signs in other parts of North Carolina advertising Lexington barbecue, but as anyone in town will tell you, to be authentic, it's got to be made by roasting pork shoulder over a wood fire in Lexington. And that's just the way it is.

The Furniture Capital

High Point is mostly about manufacturing and selling furniture. The town, already active in the lumber business, first got into furniture building in the early 1880s when a local lumber salesman noticed the big difference between the price of wood as it left the sawmill and the price it brought once it had been shipped away and turned into furniture. Sensibly, he and two local merchants risked all they had to start a furniture company close to the source of the wood. It was the right idea in the right place at the right time. Sales took off and the future was set. Today High Point has 125 furniture manufacturing companies.

Unless you are professionally involved in the furniture business, avoid High Point in April and October, when for the better part of two weeks in both months the town hosts the Southern Furniture Market, usually referred to simply as "market." Said to be the largest furniture show in the world (it fills 150 buildings and between five and six million square feet), this trade show attracts interior decorators and furniture retailers—in other words *buyers*—from all over the world. More than 1,500 furniture company exhibitors show up for each market show. Multiply that by the staff each company brings to work the booths and add all the buyers who come looking for the latest goodies, and you get an image of a town, normal population on the shy side of 70,000, so overloaded that if it were a ship it would sink. Finding a place to stay or to eat is a challenge.

The rest of the time, High Point is an interesting place where you can enjoy some terrific furniture bargains. The town also has some unusual attractions. The **Angela Peterson Doll and Miniature Museum,** located in the Wesleyan Arms Retirement Center, 1911 North Centennial Street (919-884-2222), is unique.

So is Mrs. Peterson. Her collection of something over one thousand dolls and a half-dozen furnished dollhouses is housed in this retirement center where she lives. How Mrs. Peterson and her collection came to be here is a story in itself.

Mrs. Peterson was living in Ohio when she decided it was time to move to a retirement center. "I knew it was the rest of my life, so I wanted to choose carefully," she said. She compiled a list of sixty-eight centers meeting her criteria: being in an area with changing season, not being high rise, being affordable, and having room to take her within two years. Gradually she narrowed the list to six possibilities. A preacher from Wesleyan Arms happened to visit her during his travels in Ohio, and Mrs. Peterson says, "When he saw my dolls, he about dropped his teeth." He urged her to come to Wesleyan Arms and bring her dolls. Agreeing to give her collection to the center in exchange for being allowed to "play" with the dolls for the rest of her life, Mrs. Peterson moved to Wesleyan Arms in 1979. They took partitions out of five Sunday school rooms to create museum space, and it took Mrs. Peterson a year to get all the dolls' costumes washed and starched and set up the displays. Although not extensively promoted, the museum attracted 3,000 visitors in 1989. One local tourism official calls it the best tourist attraction in North Carolina.

Mrs. Peterson says that the collection is not large by museum standards but that it is "choice." One doll, named Eric, was given to her by her father for Christmas. He said to her, "You're a big girl now, so this will be your last doll. I paid a big price for it." The price was $4. Recently the Eric doll was appraised at $800. Another doll, which Mrs. Peterson bought in 1938 for $6.50, is now worth $2,000. Incidentally, Eric, the doll, once had a different name. Mrs. Peterson can't remember what it was, but she renamed the doll after her son, Eric.

The museum includes the biggest collection of antique religious dolls in the country—about fifty, Mrs. Peterson says. She searched them out for thirty-four years in nine countries on three continents. So little was known about crèche dolls that she went to Catholic University and spent several afternoons in the library to learn more.

Also in the collection are rag dolls, portrait dolls, dolls only a quarter-inch tall, and old and new paper dolls. Mrs. Peterson's dollhouses and her miniature collection are her second love. One of the dollhouses is a beautifully executed replica of her childhood home. There also are a country store, a ladies' emporium, and a hundred-plus-year-old log cabin.

The museum is open from 1:30 P.M. to 4:30 P.M., Tuesday, Wednesday, Thursday, and Sunday. Closed Thanksgiving, Christmas, New Year's Day, Easter, Fourth of July, and when schools are closed because of bad weather. Admission free. If you would like to talk to Mrs. Peterson, be sure to call ahead. She spends a lot of time in the museum and loves to talk about the dolls, but she sometimes needs to stay home and rest. "My arthritis slows me down," she said, "but my mouth and my mind are fine."

Another valuable museum is the **Springfield Museum of Old Domestic Art,** established in 1935 in the third meetinghouse of the Springfield Meeting, 555 East Springfield Road (919-889-4911). Museums, like history books, tend to focus on extraordinary events, wars, and politics and not on the commonplaces of day-to-day life. This museum is an exception. Here you can inspect the artifacts of daily life that were used in the neighborhood for the past 200 years or more—spinning equipment, utensils, farm items, clothing, pictures from homes, toys, and a slew of fascinating odds and ends. The curator, Brenda Haworth, says, "Most of what we have has been donated by local Quakers. It's not organized yet, but I'm working on it."

Mrs. Haworth likes to emphasize most of the items that were so commonplace in their day, objects crudely made to fill an immediate need. If you didn't know how many of them had been used, you probably could never figure out what they were for. Such artifacts simply cannot be replaced.

One example is the log lifter. It looks like a crutch for a giant. Log lifters were devices created to get logs from the ground to high points in the walls when building log cabins. One man stood at each end of the log with a lifter and heaved.

Another example is a homemade Noah's Ark, with all the animals two-by-two. This was a Sunday toy, made during the time when children in the community weren't allowed to play on Sundays with their regular toys or do much else. It was carved about one hundred years ago by Yardley Warner for his twins, probably because he sympathized with the children's rest-lessness and wanted to make them a religious toy to keep them occupied on Sundays.

Another uncommon exhibit is the 4-foot-long tin horn the coachman blew at each stop of the stagecoach along the Old Plank Road. The number of blasts blown told people at upcoming stops, such as Nathan Hunt Tavern, what passengers would be wanting when they got there. Old Plank Road was built between Fayetteville and Winston-Salem by laying down boards next to one another to form a firm-surfaced highway. Part of the old road is now Main Street. A plank from the road and a notched mile marker are also in the display. A traveler in the dark could stop at the marker and feel the number of notches on it to know how far it was to Nathan Hunt Tavern. A model shows a stagecoach on a plank road with markers to give you an idea how it all worked.

As Brenda Haworth observes, visiting here is more like going into an attic than a museum. "There's so much stuff and you can handle it. You don't get the feeling of things resting on velvet that you can't touch," she says. The museum is open by appointment. Admission free.

The High Point Historical Museum at 1805 East Lexington Avenue (919-885-6859), exhibits more traditional kinds of material related to the town's history, including military displays. There also are a display of old telephones that takes you back to before Ma Bell, a collection of furniture made in High Point, and, appropriately, woodworking tools that take you back to the first manufacturing in town. Also on the property are the restored 1786 John Haley House, a weaving house, and a blacksmith shop. Demonstrations are offered in these buildings on weekends. Museum open Tuesday through Saturday, 10:00 A.M. to 4:30 P.M., and Sunday, 1:00 to 4:30 P.M. Other buildings open only on weekends. Admission free.

A pleasant place to stay while you're in High Point is The Premier, a six-room bed and breakfast inn at 1001 Johnson Street (919-889-8349). It's a completely renovated 1907 neocolonial home in the center of High Point's historic district. The house used to be known as Mrs. Jones' house and accommodated female school teachers in what were considered modest quarters then. The ladies would scarcely recognize the place today.

The decor is luxurious and eclectic, reflecting the taste of a good designer with a flash of humor. Old botanical prints and Dali prints hang side by side in rooms with classic quilts, Oriental rugs, antique wicker, and comfortable contemporary chairs. The colors lean toward pastels, grays, and white, with surprising splashes of turquoise. In one downstairs bedroom, four huge white posts that were originally part of the side porch mark the four corners of a luxuriously festooned bed. The posts are painted so that blooming vines seem to grow toward the ceiling.

Peggy Buchanan, the innkeeper, says the inn's special mark is service—not just routine graciousness, but doing special, unexpected little things for guests, such as having a fire in the fireplace in the room, a bottle of a guest's favorite wine chilling, or a packet of exotic bubble bath for the tub.

Breakfast is lavish, with lots of fresh fruit, the inn's now-famous French toast (one version of which has Bailey's Irish

Cream in the batter), and other out-of-the-ordinary entrees.

Partly because of the efforts of a previous innkeeper, the house is surrounded with good perennial borders, so that you enjoy peonies, foxglove, daisies, and the like, brightening the area along the privet hedge.

The inn has attracted celebrities but has done it so quietly that folks didn't know they were in town. Cher is reported to have stayed here. While it's easy to see that she would enjoy the inn, one wonders what in the world she was doing in High Point in the first place.

Within walking distance of the inn, you can dine at J. Basul Noble's, at 114 South Main Street (919-889-3354), a restaurant described by one local resident as "Nouvelle American but kind of French and almost four-star." You'll find such offerings as grilled salmon with lobster sauce, veal with chef's sauce, and game such as quail or pheasant, always prepared interestingly. The restaurant has a full liquor license. Open Monday through Wednesday, 6:00 to 10:00 P.M., and Thursday through Saturday, 6:00 to 11:00 P.M.

Off the Beaten Path in The Lower Piedmont

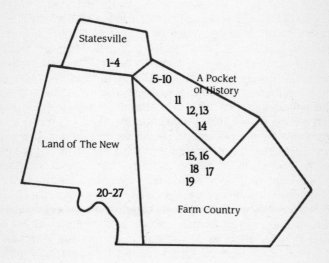

Statesville

1-4

5-10

A Pocket of History

11

12, 13

14

Land of The New

15, 16

18 17

19

20-27

Farm Country

1. Farm House Gardens
2. Eastway Deli and Cafe
3. Gluttons
4. The Arts and Science Center
5. Historic Salisbury
6. Dr. Josephus Hall House
7. Rowan Museum
8. Waterworks Visual Arts Center
9. Rowan Oak House
10. The 1868 Stewart-Marsh House
11. Kluttz Piano Factory
12. Rockwell
13. Darrell's Bar-BQ
14. Greendale

15. Motel Restaurant
16. Richfield Farm Supply
17. Cline's Country Antiques
18. The Buffalo Ranch Trading Post
19. Reed Gold Mine
20. The Homeplace
21. The Inn on Providence
22. Mint Museum of Art
23. Hezekiah Alexander Homesite
24. Discovery Place
25. The Pewter Rose
26. Dilworth Brewing Company
27. Schiele Museum of Natural History and Planetarium

The Lower Piedmont

Statesville

In less than an hour, you can drive west on Interstate 40 from Winston-Salem to Statesville, where you'll find several delightful stops known mostly to local folks. **Farm House Gardens** is on the east side of town on Highway 70 (704-873-2057). If you like gardening and houseplants, you'll find that you simply must buy some plants here, even if it means driving five hundred miles home with them in the back seat. Kay Kincaid, the main Farm House gardener, started the business about ten years ago with the encouragement of her husband, Randy, as the obvious expression of her lifelong passion for plants. "I always loved plants. So did my mother and before her, my grandmother. When I was little, I spent all my time around the farm at my grandmother's knees in the garden," she says. The force of that passion produced a nursery-greenhouse-gift shop combination that stuns you with the variety and quality of the offerings. This isn't the kind of place where anybody counts the number of plants for sale or measures in terms of how many greenhouses are open (that number changes with the seasons anyway). Farm House Gardens surely isn't the largest retail plant operation in North Carolina, but it is the place you go for the special plants you haven't been able to find anywhere else. In spring, you can buy tomato plants and pepper plants, but that's rather like choosing peanut butter in a gourmet shop. The perennials fill benches and the space under them and are lined up along the paths of the back gardens. In the greenhouses, houseplants, including little myrtle topiaries and several different maidenhair ferns, tempt you to exceed your budget with every step you take. All the common herbs and many more that are hard to find are here too, along with Japanese maples in great variety, enough different hostas to fill a small catalog, and rare dwarf shrubs. One gardener, nursing sore feet the day after a visit to Farm House Gardens, complained that she'd been there for four hours and hadn't seen everything.

As if the variety weren't enough, you deal with people who so obviously love and know the plants that it's more like swapping cuttings with Aunt Elizabeth than a commercial transaction. If you mistakenly zero in on a not-for-sale stock plant and are crushed that you can't have it, Kay or one of her helpers will cut off a little start for you and tuck it into the soil of another plant you've purchased along with instructions, if you need them, on how to root the slip. If you're one who boasts that you have a black thumb and can kill anything, don't go here. They mean for your plants to thrive, and any other attitude would be an insult. Open 9:00 A.M. to 5:00 P.M., Monday through Saturday. Closed Sunday. Write Route 7, Box 27, Statesville, 28677.

After all that walking, you'll have earned a bite to eat. Two nearby possibilities are fun. If you continue on Highway 70 toward Statesville, at a small complex called Eastway Plaza (1417 Salisbury Road) you'll find the **Eastway Deli and Cafe,** where you can indulge in an exotic sandwich and a bottle of imported beer or a glass of tea, surrounded by local gentlefolk who stop in for a leisurely lunch with Mama or a friend. You may see a three-generation gathering or a group of matrons in sporty clothing. The dining room has lots of philodendrons, travel posters on the walls, and low-backed white booths, creating a relaxed, cheery atmosphere. The most popular items on the menu are subs and carrot cake. Juniper spiral topiary plants outside the door set the entrance apart in a most un-deli-like manner. Open Monday through Saturday, 8:00 A.M. to 6:00 P.M.; closed Sunday (702-872-3700).

A more elaborate alternative for lunch or dinner attracts you even with its name, **Gluttons** (704-872-6951). Lots of young business people eat here. The place is trendy and a little noisy but always full of activity and fun. The copper tabletops rest on old treadle sewing machine bases. Stained glass and some wall decorations that look like they're hand drawn on rice paper, though they're not, provide you with interesting things to look at in every direction. Sometimes after dinner a roving magician stops at your table to pull off some very convincing sleight of hand.

As for the menu, lots of fresh salads and homemade dressings help ease your conscience if you go for the chef's special pork ribs or the Garden Sampler, fresh garden vegetables batter fried and served with a dipping sauce. Other possibilities include wings fixed in several different ways, steaks, and broiled seafood and chicken. Gluttons has Killian's Irish Red beer on tap and offers good wines by the glass. To get there, take the Broad Street exit off Interstate 77 to Newton Plaza (1539 East Broad Street). Open for lunch, Monday through Friday, 11:30 A.M. to 2:30 P.M., and for dinner,

Monday through Saturday, 5:00 to 10:00 P.M.

Don't leave Statesville without seeing **The Arts and Science Center,** 1335 Museum Road. This is a truly local museum, and the story of its beginning and growth makes you feel good. The center is housed in a turn-of-the-century building that was the Statesville waterworks until 1940. In 1956 a group of local citizens decided that the area needed a museum and put their energy and money into making it happen. Today it operates with a $100,000-a-year budget that allows for three full-time professionals on the staff. Enthusiasm for it practically shoots out the ears of Cynthia Hanson, the director. The museum features ten temporary exhibits a year, runs thirty-five educational programs in association with the local school system each year, and displays three thousand objects in the permanent collection. The glassware pieces number over a thousand. Cynthia says the quality of the items varies, but she feels it's important to have it all. "Somebody has to save all those Avon pieces," she says. Plans for the future include identifying all the glassware. A geologist has already put in a marathon rock-identification day to tag and group the five hundred rocks in the collection.

In the small toy-and-doll collection, you'll see a Victorian doll with brown eyes—a rarity, because Queen Victoria had blue eyes, and most dolls were modeled on her.

One of the museum's founders insisted that it deal with science as well as art to attract people not interested in the arts. To help fill that need, two partly restored pioneer cabin sites have been included.

Cynthia gets most excited about the art exhibits. "We're getting really good quality exhibits because the setting is so wonderful—a pretty spot on thirty-five acres in the Piedmont by a creek." The staff has high hopes of getting an exhibit by Dr. Selma Burke, a well-known black sculptor in her late eighties, who was born nearby in Mooresville. Cynthia also plans to put together an exhibit on art in the work place that will be created by asking industry to supply products to use in collages and other works.

But what captures the imagination of the public here is the homeless mummy. Well, it has a home now, but nobody has been able to say for sure how it got there. They know she died when she was thirty-five years old, that her remains are two thousand years old, and that she was mummified at a time when practitioners were getting a little sloppy about the process, but all

Cynthia knows about her recent history is that the museum and the mummy have both been there since 1956. Nobody knows where the mummy came from before that. Cynthia said, "A lot of the people involved are still alive, but not all of them remember where the trucking company went to get things. One woman who might know has long since moved, and we can't find her."

The best rumor about the mummy is that another museum rejected it because it was cursed. Maybe it was a good curse. Good things certainly have been happening while Ms. Mummy lives at The Arts and Science Center. Open Tuesday through Friday, 10:00 A.M. to 5:00 P.M.; Saturday, 10:00 A.M. to 4:00 P.M.; and Sunday, 1:00 to 4:00 P.M. Closed Monday (704) 873-4734).

A Pocket of History

Now head east on Highway 70 for twenty or thirty minutes to **Historic Salisbury.** Two kinds of people live here—those whose families have been in place for generations and those who have moved in recently, mostly from up north. Both share an almost smug conviction that theirs is one of the most congenial, historically interesting communities in North Carolina. I say *almost* smug because they're right. Although this is one of the oldest towns in the area, and the entire 23-block downtown community of commercial and residential buildings dating from 1820 to 1920 is on the National Register of Historic Places, it receives relatively little attention from outside. The Historic Salisbury Foundation and an active group of supporters are trying to change that.

They point to the 1898 Grimes Mill, a roller mill with all its original machinery in five floors; the Civil War Salisbury Confederate Prison Site and National Cemetery, where the largest number of unknown Civil War soldiers are buried; and the restored Railroad Depot. All of them are open to the public.

Then there's the Historic Salisbury walking tour that includes the homes in the National Register Historic District. Some of these homes are open to the public. The **Dr. Josephus Hall House,** 226 South Jackson Street, for instance, is a large, 1820, antebellum house that sits among old oaks and boxwoods that have been in place nearly as long as the house. Dr. Hall was chief surgeon at the Salisbury Confederate Prison during the Civil War. After the war, the Union commander used the house as headquarters.

Somehow the grounds and the interior escaped the destruction typically associated with Yankee occupation in the south, and the Hall House contains nearly all its original furnishings. Open Saturday and Sunday, 2:00 to 5:00 P.M. Modest admission fee (704-636-0103).

Also on Jackson Street, the **Rowan Museum,** in the 1819 Judge James Martin House, has hand-carved Stirewalt mantels, magnificent woodwork and trim, and a spiral staircase that curves up for three floors to an impressive ceiling medallion. The museum contains collections of early Rowan County history and several rooms furnished in the style of the period with work by Rowan craftsmen. Open Thursday through Sunday, 2:00 to 5:00 P.M. Closed legal holidays. Modest admission fee charged (704-633-5946).

Moving from the historic to the contemporary, the **Waterworks Visual Arts Center,** at the corner of West Kerr and Water Street, features changing exhibits of contemporary art. The outdoor sculpture garden is especially pleasant on clear, sunny days. The gallery is in a building that was first used as the Salisbury Waterworks and then as the city police station. Its large open spaces are especially suited to displaying art. Open Tuesday through Friday, 10:00 A.M. to 5:00 P.M.; Saturday, 9:00 A.M. to 4:00 P.M.; and Sunday, 1:00 to 4:00 P.M. Closed Mondays. Nominal donation suggested.

In downtown Salisbury, which you really must see for its remarkable old factory and business buildings, you can break the fast-food habit by having a bite of lunch at Spanky's, an old-fashioned ice cream parlor that serves not only homemade ice cream concoctions, but also good soups, salads, deli sandwiches, and cheesecake (704-638-0780). Spanky's actually makes seventy-five different flavors of ice cream, but the owner explained, almost apologetically, that they keep only twenty-five flavors on hand at a time! The restaurant is in an old building that in 1859 was the tallest in North Carolina. Open Monday through Saturday, 9:00 A.M. to 8:00 P.M., and Sunday, noon to 8:00 P.M.

When you're ready to spend the night, you have two nice bed and breakfast alternatives, each quite different from the other. At **Rowan Oak House,** 208 Fulton Street, Bill and Ruth Ann Coffey pamper and feed you outrageously in the Victorian elegance of their 1902 Queen Anne house (704-633-2086). The Coffeys have worked steadily at improving the property, returning the landscaping to more authentically Victorian gardens and maintaining the remarkably intact interior, where the original wallpaper is still in perfect condition.

Ruth Ann's gourmet breakfasts, which always include fantastic homemade breads, won't win the Weight Watchers' prize for moderation, but they're worth the splurge, the more so because the meal comes to you on Wedgwood, served with real silver and linen. Bill and Ruth Ann have worked most of their lives with people; they talk easily and interestingly and have the knack of knowing when you don't feel like talking. All the rooms have private baths. One has a two-person whirlpool.

Gerry and Charles Webster offer less ornate but equally historical accommodations in their Federal home, **The 1868 Stewart-Marsh House** (220 South Ellis Street, 704-633-6841). The guest rooms are unusually spacious and have ceiling fans as well as private baths. The parlor is simple and quite formal. The pine-paneled den with its fireplace is comforting and cozy. Visitors are fascinated with the 3-foot-by-7-foot pocket window in the front of the house that has more than thirty little panes, all still the original glass.

The overall effect is of light, airy simplicity. Gerry says they've tried to keep the atmosphere appropriate to the house, which was not elaborate because it was built right after the Civil War when nobody had much money to spend on houses.

Breakfast at the 1868 Stewart-Marsh House features seasonal fruits and Gerry's imaginative entrees. One favorite is a casserole of grits, cheese, and sausage, which she serves with fried apples and coffee cake muffins.

Whichever place you choose, have Ruth Ann or Gerry try to arrange a dinner for you in Lee Piper's home. Lee caters and also prepares special meals by reservation only that she serves to you in the dining room of the old family home, where all the crystal, china, and silver she uses come right out of the family cupboards. You sit on an elegant Victorian couch that to Lee is simply the couch the family always had in the parlor. Family photos and artwork by family members and friends hang on the walls.

After Lee's father died, the house became hers, and she'll tell you that he's still there. Not in memory, not in photographs, not in spirit, unless you think of ghosts as spirits, but in person. She and friends who've stayed there tell many stories about a presence in the hall, a favorite rocking chair of Father's that sometimes rocks, doors that open and close, and so on. They agree it's a little strange, but Lee thinks it is OK to have him there. "He just wants to see that I'm all right," she says.

There's nothing ephemeral about Lee's cooking. She'll prepare what you want—Greek, French, Indian, Chinese. When you come for an Indian dinner, she opens the door dressed in a sari. Having traveled widely, she has taught herself to remember and dupli-cate the things she tastes along the way. She doesn't have any-thing against cookbooks, but she doesn't really need them. Her house is a short walk from either bed and breakfast, so you don't even have to get in the car to get there.

When you're ready to leave Salisbury, take Highway 52 south for an interesting drive that shows you the down-home, not the tourist, version of the Piedmont. In about 6 miles, almost before you've left Salisbury's environs, you come to Granite Quarry, where a big billboard on the left side of the road directs you to **Kluttz Piano Factory.** They deliver free, but probably not if you live in Cincinnati. Stop in and look around, even though you probably aren't looking to buy a piano while you're out tracking unbeaten paths. This place, which advertises over five hundred new and rebuilt pianos, is awesome. The showroom where you try out new and reconditioned pianos, looks fairly standard, but you'll be dumbfounded by the work area that seems roughly the size of a football field, filled with pianos, whole pianos, and pieces of pianos in every make, model, and size. Ten minutes of just looking will tell you more about what's inside a piano than you've ever dreamed you could know. The people who work here talk as casually about the good and bad traits of grands and uprights and spinets and Yamahas and Wurlitzers and Baldwins as the rest of us talk about the tomatoes in our gardens.

Outsiders sometimes get a chuckle out of the name *Kluttz*, but around here, Kluttz is just another family name, belonging not only to the owners of the piano factory, but also to archi-tects, contractors, and art shop proprietors. Everybody works hard, even the older Mr. Kluttz, who thinks nothing of being one of two men to haul a grand piano off its legs, out of a truck, and into a house. You'll notice some of the people wear big gold belt buckles shaped like grand pianos. Ask about the buckles, and the only answer you'll get is, "It means we're special." Some workers get there as early as 4:00 A.M., but regular hours for ordinary mortals are Monday through Friday, 8:00 A.M. to 5:00 P.M., and Saturday, 8:00 A.M. to 3:00 P.M. (704-279-7237).

Continuing on Highway 52 south, which is really going east at this point, brings you to **Rockwell,** which you should pronounce ROCKwul, not RockWELL. The town bears no relationship to Norman Rockwell, but it should: flags fly from all the porches on Memorial Day; signs advertise "bait, crickets and night crawlers"; women still appear occasionally with their hair in curlers; neighbors stop each other in the grocery store to ask if the new "granbaby" has arrived yet; pink and blue bows on mailboxes announce when the new grans do come into the world. Stop for some good, authentic barbecue at **Darrell's Bar-BQ** in Rockwell. If you call ahead, you can even pick it up at a drive-through window, although then you'll miss the chance to mingle with the local people inside (704-279-6300). Darrell's is open Tuesday through Saturday, 10:00 A.M. to 9:00 P.M. Closed Sunday and Monday.

Back on Highway 52 and driving southeast again, you'll pass a couple of permanent yard-sale junk shops, a tattoo shop, a few roadside taverns, and lots of modest country homes, some in dreadful disarray and some perfectly kept with geraniums and picket fences. About 10 miles beyond Rockwell, you'll come to Holts Service and County Line Motors—used-car lot, gas stop, and beer store. Inside you can almost always find a few folks sitting around sipping Miller Lite or Budweiser—the local preferences—gossiping or playing cards. You can have a beer on the spot or buy a six to take out. Whether you stop or not, use this landmark to find the turn from Highway 52 onto Old Beatty Ford Road for an hour's diversion down a rural entrepreneurial row. The best way to be sure you don't miss it is to drive to Holts, turn around and backtrack a few seconds to where you'll see the Old Beatty Ford sign, and turn left onto a road that crosses the railroad tracks and runs past a large quarry operation. You'll drive about a dozen miles along this road, past a Soil Conservation Service demonstration farm on the left, a home-based sewing machine repair shop called "Sew and Sew," another home business, "Why Knot Upholstery," and Miller Farms Racing (a track around grassy fields). Among these little businesses, many yards have for-sale signs offering produce in season, a piece of used farm equipment, a boat, a camper "like new" with tow bar and a pickup (there must be a story in that one), firewood, oil paintings—it all changes with fortune and the seasons. You'll also pass a couple of uncommonly attractive older churches, the kind with their own manicured graveyards in back. Old Concord Road intersects Old Beatty Ford Road after about 12 miles. Turn left. Drive about 3 miles more, passing Roy Cline Road and Irish Potato Road to turn right immediately onto Goldfish Road. You're at **Greendale,** which from the outside looks like one more sprawling roadside building. Inside you'll find wonder and the ultimate rural entrepreneurial enterprise.

Long rows of beautifully clear, brightly lighted aquariums gleam in the dim room. Here in the boonies, where if you tell your mother you're going to the fish store she assumes you're going to buy flounder, you discover gouramis and guppies, oscars, cichlids, corals, and saltwater exotics whose names you don't even know, all apparently thriving. OK, you can't keep goldfish on the road, but just the looking beats watching television, and you may find the selection and prices on aquarium equipment appealing enough to tease a travelers' check out of your wallet before you leave.

Greendale started out as a goldfish farm back in 1929 when Rufus Green got laid off by Cannon Mills and decided to make his living raising goldfish in outdoor ponds to sell to dime stores. One of his first sales was to get money to buy a shirt for church. As years passed, Rufus died, and his wife maintained the business as well as she could. Rufus's son, George, returned in 1978 from another war that wasn't called one, with his wife, Gaysorn, a classical dancer from Bangkok. By now hobbyists had turned enthusiastically to exotic tropical fish, so it made sense for Greendale to develop accordingly. The whole story, in a yellowing newspaper clipping, is taped to the front wall.

It's hard to imagine there would be enough customers to keep the business going, but they come from all directions: Concord, Kannapolis, Salisbury, Albemarle. The store is closed on Tuesdays, partly because new shipments of plants and fish come then. On Wednesdays it's so busy that, as one employee put it, "People just come in and throw money at you." They're all there, Gay and George, Mrs. Rufus Green, and local young people who work here and often get themselves hooked on the hobby in the process. You can always find someone to chat with about the troublesome habits of live bearers and how hard it is not to disrupt a gourami's bubble nest (704-933-1798). Open Monday and Wednesday through Saturday, 10:00 A.M. to 6:00 P.M., and Sunday, 2:00 to 6:00 P.M. Closed Tuesday.

When you leave, depending on which way you turn, you may see a large block-lettered sign inside a cul-de-sac in front of a mobile home: IF YOU DON'T HAVE BUSINESS HERE, THIS IS A GOOD PLACE FOR

YOU TO TURN AROUND. This may be the only guy in the county who isn't looking for customers at home. The best way to return to Highway 52 is the way you came in. Since everything looks different going in the opposite direction, you'll see things you missed the first time and won't feel that you're backtracking.

Coming into Misenhiemer, Highway 52 runs through the middle of the small Pfeiffer College campus, where all the classroom buildings, administration buildings, dormitories, and faculty houses are made of red brick. You might think that this is the kind of place a film director would like to shoot *Who's Afraid of Virginia Wolf?* although a director would never get approval in this Bible pocket. If it did happen, people would raise a big stink in the *Stanley News and Press*.

Farm Country

From Pfeiffer College it's only a couple of miles to the intersection of Highway 52 and Highway 49 at Richfield. Go north on Highway 49 for about as long as you need to take two deep breaths and pull into the parking lot of the **Motel Restaurant**. This is the breakfast and lunch spot for many of the local farmers, the people who work in the mobile home factories and the Perfect Fit textile plant down the road. For breakfast you get two eggs, bacon, grits or hash browns, biscuits or cornbread, and coffee for about $2.50. Lunch is one meat (meatloaf or fried fish, maybe, the selections are written on a blackboard at the door), two vegetables, and beverage for $3.25. Sit at the counter and you can study the ever-lengthening row of imprinted mugs: *Old Age Ain't No Place for Sissies, If God Wanted Me to Cook and Clean My Hands Would've Been Made of Aluminum, My Parents Went to Myrtle Beach* and *All they Got Me Was this Dumb Mug, God Loves You and I'm Trying*.

The Motel Restaurant waitresses know all the regulars by name, ask, "You doin' OK?" as they take your order, and after the first time, remember what it is that you always have. They like a good joke. Did you hear about the prostitute who told her tax consultant that she was a chicken farmer? Well, she said . . . Country music plays in the background, and while Willie and Waylon are appreciated, one of the waitresses says she'd really like to marry Conway, even if she is already married and he's old.

But Randy Travis, now, he's one of our own, coming from Monroe and all. When you've had all the coffee or iced tea you can hold, leave a couple quarters on the counter, pay your bill, and when someone says, "Come back," you say, "I'll do it." Open Monday through Friday, 5:00 A.M. to 2:00 P.M., and Saturday, 5:00 to 11:00 A.M.

Gas up at the **Richfield Farm Supply** store. Get back on Highway 52 south, go 1 block to the yellow caution light, and turn right toward Millingport on South Main Street. You'll immediately see a feed mill next to the railroad tracks, and the farm store is right there. It's a wide, low, metal building, where in addition to buying your gas you can stock up on Pepsi and Cheerwine (made in Salisbury) and pick up a local paper. You probably won't be in the market for chain saws or buckets or rope or canning jars or seed, but you can get them here too. Two or three men are usually sitting in the semicircle of chairs at the end of the counter; sometimes one or two more will be leaning against the counter. When you come through the door, they'll check to see if they know you, speak pleasantly whether they do or not, and then probably go back to watching the Pepsi sign over the door. The other day somebody said they should get Mickey and Jim to put a television up there, but nobody was serious. It's busy enough talking about who's cutting firewood and what happened to the guard fence across the railroad tracks, and for the benefit of any visiting Yankee, the best way to cook up a pot of greens.

In the winter the store, like many homes, is heated with a kerosene heater that sits there in the middle of the semicircle. It's not like the old days when you could sit around the wood-burning stove and spit. The heat's just as good, but for the rest of it you need an empty soda can. Open Monday through Saturday, 8:00 A.M. to 6:00 P.M.

From here you could take Highway 49 north through the Uhwarrie Forest back up to Asheboro, or you could go south for an interesting drive to Charlotte. Expect to have to be patient. The road is only one lane in each direction with few places to pass, and you'll probably spend some time behind a tractor or a slow-moving truck hauling logs. Even going slowly, you'll be at Mount Pleasant in ten or fifteen minutes.

Shortly before you come to the crossroads at Mount Pleasant, a sign on the right advertises **Cline's Country Antiques.** A big, rusting antique tractor marks the lane back to the seven long buildings where Don Cline manages an ever-changing stock. He buys and wholesales antiques by the truckload but attends with equal care to your $5 purchase of an old advertising sign or kitchen utensil. One of the most fascinating things you can do is ask for a particular kind of antique—an oak washstand or armoire, or a pie safe, for instance—and then watch Don reflect a minute before he directs you, without consulting any kind of inventory list at all, to the precise building and corner in which you'll find what you're looking for. No one's quite sure how he does it, but no matter how often or how fast his inventory changes, Don always knows where everything is.

His appearance reflects the fact that Don detests malls and spending money on glitzy new things; he prides himself on living out of his junk. His britches came from a load the pickers hauled in, his sweater was in a bin of post office surplus that he found at a dumpster, and his Sunday suit was part of the stock he got when he bought all the remaining merchandise of a department store that went out of business several years ago.

If he's not out supervising the coming and going of truckloads, Don will probably be sitting in the old barber chair by the wood stove in the barn talking with visiting dealers or reading old issues of antiques magazines. A couple of years ago, Don collaborated with a professional writer on the book, *Buying and Selling Antiques*. Across from Don's barber chair, Vichard, his assistant, nailed up a wooden box to hold copies of the book, with a sign above that reads THE BOOK and an arrow pointing down to the copies that are for sale.

The idea of Don's writing a book seems surprising when you first encounter his plain-old-country-boy demeanor, but pay attention, ask a few questions, and you'll learn that he has taught economics in a couple of area colleges, has a photographic memory, and is perfectly willing to let you think he's stupid if you're so inclined because it helps business. Not that he's dishonest; he won't sell an imperfect piece without pointing out the flaw, he won't knowingly misrepresent anything, and he charges only a modest markup on his merchandise. Don Cline may be the most scrupulously honest antiques dealer in the business, but he doesn't see any reason to rouse your jousting instincts by flaunting his brain.

Actually, in the beginning he wasn't that eager to go into business at all. It's just that he loved auctions and couldn't resist good buys. When he got married, his wife pointed out that unless he started moving stuff out at something close to the speed with which he brought it in, there wasn't going to be room for her. Then too, there on his father's farm were all those long chicken sheds, empty since the cholesterol scare made producing eggs unprofitable. All the setup really needed was customers, so Don began to let it be known that he had some stuff to sell. The rest, as they say, is history. Cline's Country Antiques (704-436-6824) is open from sometime around 8:00 A.M. or 9:00 A.M. to sometime about dark, Tuesday through Saturday. Closed Sunday and Monday.

If you get to hanging around the Cline place so late you don't feel like driving anymore, you could stay at the Patriot Inn in Mount Pleasant. This is a simple, clean, quiet motel, with a sign out front pointing out how many long country miles you still have to Charlotte or Raleigh and inviting you to stay there instead. A few rooms have refrigerators. Rates are modest (704-436-9616).

When you drive on down toward Concord, you're probably going to blink and do a double take because you'll think you're seeing a herd of buffalo on the hillside. You *are* seeing buffalo. **The Buffalo Ranch Trading Post** maintains a growing number of buffalo, offers horse-drawn stagecoach rides across the fields so you can see the buffalo and deer, and invites you to walk through the kid-oriented petting zoo. Then in the exotic zoo, you'll find an extensive variety of monkeys, miniature horses, and Vietnamese potbellied pigs, among other animals. At the lake, you can feed the carp and catfish. If you bring your own tackle, you can fish too. And in the western store, which smells convincingly of leather and wooden floorboards, you can buy boots or a belt or cowboy hat or smaller souvenirs of the visit.

This unlikely Wild West spread used to belong to the Cook family. A few years ago, Mr. Cook decided it was time to sell and called the grandfather of Doug and Ken Godley. The men got together, talked for thirteen to thirty minutes, struck a deal, shook hands, and the brothers had themselves a buffalo ranch. The boys didn't know a lot about animals, but they set about learning in a hurry and now are proud of the fact that their herd is growing. They've got about twenty buffalo now and want to build the herd up to thirty or more. How do you build up a herd of buffalo? "They have babies every year," Ken said. The brothers are paying Grandfather back, business thrives, and being around the success is fun for visitors. Bring a picnic and allow yourself a little time to pitch a game of horseshoes. The Western store is open year-round. The stagecoach rides and park are available March 15 through November 15. Moderate admission fee (704-782-2009).

When you get to where Highway 601 meets Highway 49, you may decide to make a side trip on Highway 601 south to Highway 200 and follow the signs to the **Reed Gold Mine** at Stanfield, about 10 miles east of Concord (704-786-8337). This is the site of the first authenticated gold find in the United States. It seems that Conrad Reed found a gold nugget the size of a brick on his farm and after that sort of lost interest in farming. We tend to associate the gold rushes with Alaska and California, but the fever burned here in North Carolina back in the late 1820s. For a time more people worked at gold mining than any other occupation except farming. Here and there in the state you still find places such as Morning Star Explorations at Richfield where the search for more gold continues or has begun anew. At the Reed Gold Mine State Historic Site, you can pan for gold in the spring and summer and tour the mining area year-round. In the visitor center, exhibits and a film explain the history and mining process. Admission is free, but a modest fee is charged for panning. Open April 1 to October 31, Monday through Saturday 9:00 A.M. to 5:00 P.M., and Sunday, 1:00 to 5:00 P.M. Open November 1 through March 31, Tuesday through Saturday 10:00 A.M. to 4:00 P.M., and Sunday, 1:00 to 4:00 P.M. Closed Monday.

Back on Highway 49 heading south again, two little local businesses can be fun. About 3½ miles before you reach Harrisburg, the Greenway Garden Center sells a nice variety of herbs and perennials, as well as redworms and crickets for bait. You may not be planning to fish, but you'll enjoy the young people who run the place and get a sense of local flavor from such episodes as a couple of retirees walking in to donate a bushel basket of canna bulbs because they had run out of space for planting them at home. Open Monday through Friday, 9:00 A.M. to 5:00 P.M., and Saturday and Sunday, 9:00 A.M. to 4:00 P.M. Hours may be shorter in January and February (704-788-6915).

Just south of Harrisburg, the This 'n That shop carries some of the best quality handcrafted items and antiques in the area. Operating on the theory that good attracts good, Elizabeth Bailey, who used to be an elementary school teacher, has been systematically bringing in the best needlework, woodwork, and handmade dolls she can find and selling them at prices that encourage the craftspeople to continue working. The items, therefore, are not cheap, but neither are they as expensive as their counterparts in glitzy city gift shops. Elizabeth likes to talk about the people and their work and her fondness for the area.

Elizabeth came to North Carolina in 1962 from Greeneville, Tennessee. Her first love was quilting. She's found that as her business grows she hasn't much time for quilting anymore, though she likes to work out designs and take them to a woman who does an especially fine job on the actual quilting. It's not surprising that she's finding the shop time-consuming, because she looks for crafts from all over the state, not just the immediate region. The stock includes items from as far away as Thomasville, Hickory, and Lenore as well as from better-known crafts areas such as Asheville. The shop is open Tuesday through Saturday, 10:00 A.M. to 5:00 P.M., but Elizabeth warns that sometimes running a one-woman operation means she can't keep those hours perfectly. It's a good idea to call ahead if you want to be sure of visiting here.

Land of the New

Charlotte's an exciting place to visit these days. It's growing so fast that you can find something new almost every day, and everybody is feeling upbeat and turned on about it. People seem to exude civic pride. Because they're so pleased about the way things are going, they're incredibly nice to visitors. Charlotte has reason for pride: a new National Basketball Association expansion team, the Charlotte Hornets; the Charlotte Knights professional baseball team; NASCAR racing at Charlotte Motor Speedway; Douglas International Airport, with direct flights to London; a Pulitzer Prize-winning newspaper, the *Charlotte Observer;* the highly rated University of North Carolina at Charlotte; a slew of smaller colleges and universities; new skyscrapers; a new coliseum and an old coliseum. And, of course, there are Jim and Tammy Faye Bakker, earlier of PTL and Heritage U.S.A. fame, who may be the only people around who don't like Charlotte anymore.

Until Hurricane Hugo hit in the fall of 1989, Charlotte was famous for its streets lined with huge old oak trees. People called the city "The Shady Lady." Since the 90-mile-an-hour winds, things are a lot more open—including some roofs—but even before the repairs were finished, committees were planting new trees and Charlottians were looking proudly at the neighborliness and cooperation with which they handled the days- and weeks-long power outage and the physical destruction to homes, neighborhoods, and businesses. That fighting spirit, they'll tell you, has always been part of the city's heritage.

Originally the city was named for Queen Charlotte of Mecklenburg, wife of King George III, and it still calls itself "The Crown City," but the city rebelled against England in 1775 and earned from General Corwallis the complaint that Charlotte was "a hornet's nest." That historical epithet figured in naming the new NBA team the Hornets.

Charlotte's growth brings traffic, unfortunately, along with the excitement, but it would be too bad to miss some of the city's special features because of traffic. The best advice for a visitor to minimize problems is to study a city map ahead of time and try to avoid the major high-traffic highways—Interstate 85, Interstate 77, and Independence Boulevard—as much as possible. Once you're actually in the city, the traffic isn't bad, except at rush hour; it's the main arteries that clog up. Don't hesitate to ask for directions if you get confused. People seem to be used to it and are good at helping, probably because the ongoing construction everywhere has forced them to figure out new routes.

You'll find enough special places here to warrant spending a night, so perhaps you'll want to arrange for accommodations first. In addition to plenty of standard hotels and motels, Charlotte has two especially pleasant and successful bed and breakfast inns—The Homeplace, at 5901 Sardis Road, and The Inn on Providence, 6700 Providence Road. Both are on large, shady lots in residential parts of the city. The Homeplace has a gazebo in the backyard, and The Inn on Providence has a swimming pool.

At **The Homeplace** (704-365-1936), Frank and Peggy Dearien bought a restored country Victorian-style home with the requisite heart-of-pine floors, formal parlor, and 10-foot beaded ceilings. The next thing anyone knew, they were operating a bed and breakfast inn, serving bountiful breakfasts, and as a bit of lagniappe, evening desserts. The house is decorated in a soothing combination of blue and rose colors. A unique aspect of the decor is the collection of primitive paintings, painted over the past ten or so years by John Gentry, Peggy's father, with his handwritten stories on the back personalizing each one.

Darlene and Dan McNeill, at **The Inn on Providence**

(704-366-6700), offer elegant rooms in a southern homestead, furnished with early American antiques and many pieces from New England. The inn's signature is a large collection of quilts that hang on many of the long walls and cover some of the beds. The inn has a walnut-paneled library, a formal sitting room with a fireplace, and a lovely dining room with an old floor. Breakfast here focuses on Darlene's heart-shaped Norwegian waffles.

Both inns enjoy much popularity, which means steady occupancy, so it would be a good idea to make reservations well ahead of time if you'd like to try one of them.

From the southeast side of town, you can easily drive to the **Mint Museum of Art,** at 2730 Randolph Road, where exhibits celebrate both local history and world culture. The name comes from the building's having been a branch of the United States Mint in the 1800s. That made sense back when the Piedmont was producing most of the country's gold.

In 1988 the museum created a huge stir with the exhibit, "Ramses the Great: the Pharaoh and His Time," which featured, among other items, a gold statue of the pharaoh so large the building had to be modified to give him extra headroom. That exhibit is gone now, but a new permanent collection, "Spanish Colonial Art," is attracting attention. Other permanent collections include American and European paintings, African artifacts, pre-Columbian arts, costumes, and gold and currency of the Carolinas.

The Mint Museum Gift Shop specializes in offerings that reflect the museum exhibits. For instance, in connection with the pre-Columbian art exhibit, the shop sells replicas of pre-Columbian gold charms. Artifacts imported directly from African suppliers complement the museum's African displays. As the exhibits change, so do some of the gifts. A standard item in the shop that makes a nice gift is the miniature brass replica of Queen Charlotte's gold crown. A painting in which she wears the original crown hangs in a prominent position. The museum is open Tuesday, 10:00 A.M. to 10:00 P.M.; Wednesday through Saturday, 10:00 A.M. to 5:00 P.M.; and Sunday, 1:00 to 6:00 P.M. Closed Monday. Modest admission charged (704-337-2000).

Another museum in the vicinity worth your attention is the **Hezekiah Alexander Homesite** and Museum of History, at 3500 Shamrock Drive (704-568-1774). The Hezekiah Alexander house is the oldest dwelling still standing in Mecklenburg County. It was built of local quarry stone in 1774 and has been restored.

Costumed guides lead tours of the house, log kitchen, barn, and gardens. The history museum displays local crafts and artifacts. Hezekiah was a delegate to the Fifth Provincial Congress and served on the committee that drafted the North Carolina State Constitution and Bill of Rights. Admission to the museum is free; a modest fee is charged for tours. Open Tuesday through Friday, 10:00 A.M. to 5:00 P.M., and Saturday and Sunday, 2:00 to 5:00 P.M.

The Hezekiah Alexander Homesite

In uptown Charlotte at 301 North Tryon Street, the kids will enjoy **Discovery Place,** a hands-on science and technology museum where they can enjoy some close-up experiences with fish and birds, the natural sciences, and computers (704-372-6261). One of the most impressive exhibits is the tropical rain forest, which fills three stories with plants, rocks, waterfalls, and appropriate wildlife. The exhibits related to the human body are interesting too. One description claims that you learn about characteristics of the human body in a "hands-on manner," which could make you nervous if you didn't know about models and machines. Open weekdays, 9:00 A.M. to 5:00 P.M.; Saturday, 9:00 A.M. to 6:00 P.M.; and Sunday, 1:00 to 6:00 P.M. Moderate admission charged.

When you need nourishment, you might try **The Pewter Rose** at 1820 South Boulevard, close to the southeast edge of town and not difficult to reach (704-332-8149). Helen Scruggs had a small luncheon restaurant of the same name at Spirit Square in uptown Charlotte. Before opening the new and improved restaurant, she studied the culinary arts in France and then duplicated the feel with a cozy country French decor in the new Pewter Rose, in a renovated textile mill. You'll feel comfortable here in either informal or business dress, and you'll find menu items ranging from fancy burgers to some outstanding salads and platters. The smoked turkey with Béarnaise mayonnaise on orange nut bread is worth several trips across town. All the desserts, which you can order for lunch or dinner or in the bar, are homemade. You'll like the price range too, roughly $5 to $15. Open Tuesday through Friday, 11:30 A.M. to 2:00 P.M. and 6:00 to 10:00 P.M.; Saturday, 6:00 to 10:00 P.M.; barn open until midnight Friday and Saturday for coffee and desserts. Closed Sunday and Monday.

Another place that's easy to find is **Dilworth Brewing Company,** 1301 East Boulevard, where the salad, steak, and chicken menu is accompanied by a choice of several beers, porter, and ale from the microbrewery. You can see the steel workings of the brewery from the dining area. Classic French onion soup and chili are on the menu every day, along with a soup du jour. You can also order a variety of trendy snacks: nachos, buffalo wings, raw veggies, and a great beer-batter onion loaf. The Dilworth Brewing Company is very popular for lunch among people who work in the vicinity, so you might like to time your own repast to fall a little before or after the traditional noon lunch hour. Open Monday through Thursday, 11:00 A.M. to midnight, and Friday and Saturday, 11:00 A.M. to 1:00 A.M.

About 20 miles west of Charlotte in Gastonia, which you can reach quickly on Interstate 85, the **Schiele Museum of Natural History and Planetarium** attracts great numbers of visitors, especially schoolchildren, with its collection of North American mammals in habitat settings, a one hundred–seat planetarium, a restored pioneer site of the 1700s, and a Catawba Indian village. Other exhibits deal with everything from forestry to archaeology. A brochure maps out several self-guided tour suggestions for the outside grounds. Don't skip this one because it's popular; it has good reason for being so. Open Tuesday through Friday, 9:00 A.M. to 5:00 P.M., and Saturday and Sunday, 2:00 to 5:00 P.M. Planetarium shows offered only Saturday and Sunday afternoon. Admission free (704-864-3962).

Off the Beaten Path in The Mountains

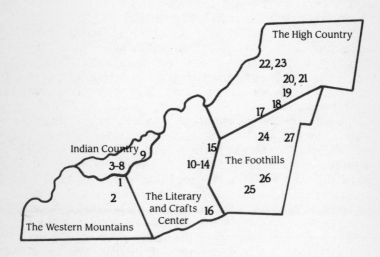

The High Country

22, 23
20, 21
19
18
17

Indian Country
3-8
9
15
10-14
The Foothills
24   27

1
26
2
The Literary
and Crafts
Center
16
25

The Western Mountains

The Mountains

The Western Mountains

Whatever you plan in the North Carolina mountains, allow about twice as much travel time as usual. Narrow roads wind through woodland and countryside, up hills so steep you sometimes feel as though your car will peel off the road backward, from hairpin turns into switchbacks followed by more curves. The squiggles don't all show on the maps, and the maps can't allow for the time it takes if you get behind a big truck with no place to pass for 50 miles. Decide ahead of time not to hurry; relax and absorb the peerless scenery.

One way to enjoy the panoramic views of mountains and valleys is by driving some part of the Blue Ridge Parkway. It stretches from Shenandoah National Park along the Blue Ridge Mountains into the southern part of the Black Mountains, through the Craggies, the Pisgahs, the Balsams, and into the Great Smokies, a total of 469 miles. The maximum speed limit along the parkway is 45 miles per hour, but in reality, traffic is often slower. It doesn't take much arithmetic to figure that it would take a long time to cover the entire length of the parkway at 30 or 40 miles perhour. The best way to plan a trip is to alternate stretches of the parkway with drives on the roads you can reach by turning off along the way. Crossovers from the parkway are marked with mileposts that are numbered and named.

Before you get on the parkway, spend some time enjoying the Nantahala National Forest, Nantahala Gorge, and Bryson City in the mountains. In Bryson City, **Randolph House,** built in 1985 by Amos Frye, is run today by his niece, Ruth Adams, and her husband, Bill, as a homey country inn. As Ruth tells it, Amos once had owned all the timber around, but when the government decided to declare most of the area national forestland, Amos had to sell. He kept the right to lumber out the sold acreage for a limited time; to get his money's worth, he set to building, using wood, of course, as fast as he could. Randolph House was one of the results.

Because the house is furnished with family antiques that have always been there, things don't all match, leaving you with the feeling that if you blink hard you'll see old Amos there in the worn leather chair. The inn's dinners are strictly by reservation because Ruth hates waste, and when you make the reservation, you choose from a list of entrees planned for that night. The cuisine might be called "Southern Gourmet," featuring choices such as Cornish hens in orange sauce and trout in pecan sauce, served perhaps with a classic southern squash casserole and a dessert of Three Hundred Dollar Chocolate Cake or Mile High Lemon Pie. Bill maintains a nice wine list. The inn is open April through October (704–488–3472).

From Bryson City, drive 9 miles southwest on Highway 19 to **Nantahala Outdoor Center** at the Nantahala Gorge. The outdoor center attracts the outdoors crowd, especially rafters and hikers. This is a congenial place to hire a guide and all the equipment you need for a white-water rafting trip down the Nantahala River. It's also great for fishing, picnicking, and hiking. Part of the fun is watching the serious rafters, who, as one observer put it, seem to have a continuing contest to see who can show up in the most worn, mismatched, clothes-don't-matter outfit. The Nantahala Outdoor Center Restaurant, right by the river, has been a popular eating place with hikers and rafters for years. Some of the most popular recipes have been bound into a cookbook, *River Runners Special,* with each recipe listed for difficulty (Class I, II, III, and so on) like the rapids on the river. Vegetarian lentil mushroom soup is Class II; amaretto cream pie is Class IV. In a recent change, the restaurant's name became River's End, to note the addition of another restaurant, Relia's Garden, at the center.

At River's End, you feel perfectly comfortable in your mismatched hiking clothes and down vest, sitting at a rustic table looking out over the river while you gobble a hearty serving of spicy beef stew with the restaurant's special herb bread. Relia's Garden is also casual, but a bit more up scale in its atmosphere and offerings. With a view of the mountains rather than the river, this restaurant sits in a field on the hill across the garden, landscaped with terraced gardens of herbs, unusual vegetables, and exotic plants. A walk through the gardens crushes fragrant bits of mint and thyme underfoot, so that no matter how hungry you were to begin with, your appetite's whetted even more by the time you go inside. Entrees range from fettuccine to prime rib. The county is dry, but brown bagging beer and wine is permitted.

Staff members of the Nantahala Outdoor Center, from guides to cooks, tend to return year after year, as do visitors. Moreover, the presence of the family that started the center is still much in evidence. Relia's Garden, for instance, is named for Arelia, wife of the founder and for many years director of food service. Her plants fill the terrace gardens. Spending time here feels like being part of an extended family or a close community. It is special. The center and restaurants operate from roughly mid-March to November 1, depending on the weather. River's End is open daily, 7:00 A.M. to 9:00 P.M. Relia's Garden serves breakfast from 7:00 to 11:00 A.M. and dinner from 5:00 to 9:00 P.M., on weekends in April and daily from May to November. In the colder months, hours may be cut back. For information about the time you plan to be here, phone (704) 488-2175.

Just a few miles (a long walk or a short ride) beyond the outdoor center, Nantahala Village offers a less strenuous and very agreeable alternative approach to the river, the gorge, and the forest. Built before the white-water craze as a rustic resort in the woods, Nantahala Village has simple rooms in the inn and a variety of cozy cabins built of logs or native stone, with knotty pine interiors. The cabins have kitchens; some have fireplaces. The dining room in the inn serves inexpensive Thanksgiving-like meals in a pleasant, though not formal, atmosphere. Windows in the dining room look out into the woods. When it's cold, a fire burns in the huge native stone fireplace.

In addition to rafting and fishing, the inn offers swimming, badminton, hiking, tennis, volleyball, Ping-Pong, and horseshoes. And for walking rather than hiking, you can't do better than the old abandoned road that winds down behind the inn for miles. Everyone, from Brad Walker, the innkeeper, to the waitresses and the activities staff, is friendly and helpful in a low-key way. Brad's wife runs Simple Pleasures, a pretty antiques and gift shop in the inn. Open April 1 to October 31. The opening and closing dates may vary (704-488-2826).

Indian Country

Picking up the Blue Ridge Parkway at Cherokee brings you to some decisions about the kind of tourist you mean to be. The town, in the **Qualla Boundary Cherokee Indian Reservation** where Highways 441 and 19 meet, maintains several features dedicated to preserving and explaining the history of the Cherokee nation, which was nearly wiped out by the infamous "Trail of Tears" forced walk in 1838, when the U.S. government tried to relocate all Indians to west of the Mississippi River. Some of the Cherokees escaped the march by hiding in the hills.

Eventually they were able to return to this area where they were once the powerful Cherokee nation. Their story is told in *Unto These Hills,* an outdoor drama played by a cast of 130 people, beginning between 8:00 and 9:00 P.M. nightly, except Sunday, from mid-June through late August, in an outdoor theater that seats 2,800 people. The program is presented by the Cherokee Historical Association with support from the Theatre Arts Section of the North Carolina Arts Council and funds appropriated by the North Carolina General Assembly. The story begins with DeSoto's arrival in 1540 and climaxes with the Trail of Tears exodus. Many of the players are descendants of the Cherokee who lived the story. Moderately high admission fee. Box office (704–497–2111) open from 9:00 A.M. to 10:00 P.M. during the summer season and from 9:00 A.M. to 4:30 P.M. in the off-season. The story and performance are frankly moving; it's not uncommon to see people in the audience cry.

Unfortunately, activities of this caliber are surrounded by the tourist-tacky pseudo-Indian concessions that seem to plague the areas around Indian populations across the country. Trying to sort out the authentic and the merely exploitative can be depressing. You can count on quality at the **Cherokee Cyclorama Wax Museum** and **Oconaluftee Indian Village,** which are also sponsored by the Cherokee Historical Association, where the Cherokee history has been told with life-sized dioramas, recorded narrations, and an electronic map. The Oconaluftee Indian Village, a living replication of a 1750s Cherokee Village, shows you Indians practicing their historical crafts of basket making, pottery, canoe building, food preparations, and weaponry, and perhaps even more important, explaining the culture within which these activities proceeded. Hour-long tours begin every five minutes, but you are not locked into them and there is plenty of time for exploring, photographing, and questioning. Open 9:00 A.M. to 5:30 P.M., May through October. Moderately high admission charge (704–497–2111).

Qualla Arts and Crafts Mutual, Inc., the most successful Indian-owned and -operated craft cooperative in the country, at the entrance of the *Unto These Hills* theater on Highway 441, offers you an opportunity to buy genuine Indian beadwork, baskets, wood carvings, pots, masks, and the like. Cherokee work is displayed in separate rooms from that of other tribes. Open Monday through Saturday, 8:00 A.M. to 6:00 P.M., and Sunday, 8:00 A.M. to 5:00 P.M. (704-497-3103).

Finally, the **Museum of the Cherokee Indian** (704-497-3481) displays traditional arts and crafts and offers a video on the history of the nation, along with displays of tools and various accounts of the Trail of Tears journey. Open daily, 9:00 A.M. to 5:30 P.M., later during the summer. Modest admission charged. Closed Thanksgiving, Christmas, and New Year's Day. For full information about attractions, contact the Cherokee Travel Center (704-497-9195).

Cherokee is considered the gateway to the Great Smoky Mountains, and it seems important to mention, however briefly, the Great Smoky Mountains National Park, established in 1934 partly with money donated by John D. Rockefeller. The park merits a full book in itself: elevations climb as you move along the northeast; plant life, wildlife, and scenery invite superlatives; the bears and the weather are unpredictable. About half the park falls in Tennessee, but North Carolinians, figuring there's plenty for all, forgive that. Staying on the North Carolina side, you'll find enough hiking, fishing, and camping to last most of your life without being repetitious. There are several visitor centers in the park. For information, call (616) 436-5615. It's a Tennessee number, but it's also park headquarters and the best place to start when you need advance information. The park is said to have attracted more than ten million visitors a year in recent years, mostly in the summer. Although with about 500,000 acres to explore, there'd seem to be enough room for everyone, you'll probably enjoy your visit more if you avoid the peak summer season.

Your next major stop should probably be Asheville, altitude 2,250 feet, population just under 60,000. You can amble along the Blue Ridge Parkway to get there, or go more directly along Highway 19. Either way, you might detour onto Highway 23 to stop in **Waynesville** (you are now at altitude 3,000 feet), a little town of Scotch-Irish and English founding where travelers like to stop to get away from the obvious tourist attractions and enjoy some real people. Waynesville is the home of the annual ramps festival. The ramp is a rank, onionlike, wild plant of no particular virtue, except that every summer the people of Waynesville have a big party to cook it all the ways they can think of: steamed ramps, braised ramps, ramps a la king, ramps fritters. Presumably, somebody eats the results, but that is not as conspicuous as the cooking, which leaves a garlicky odor heavy on the town all day. For some reason, it's a popular time and place for politicians to appear. If you'd like to spend a night and have dinner in congenial, rustic surroundings here, try Grandview Lodge, owned and operated by Stanley and Linda Arnold (704-456-5212). The Arnolds are actually newcomers, escapees from corporate Chicago. The inn has been operating for the past fifty-plus years; the Arnolds took it over as part of a longtime dream in 1986. Linda's cooking, which emphasizes fresh produce and herbs, whole-grain flours, and homemade desserts, has been so popular that she published a cookbook, *The Grandview Lodge Cookbook*, for guests who hope to duplicate some of her meals at home. Stanley loves to play bridge: if you were to show up as a threesome looking for a fourth, you'd win his heart forever. Stan has another talent that fits interestingly into the Waynesville scene. He speaks Polish, Russian, German, and Hebrew. In recent years Waynesville has become known for international folk-dance festivals—which gives Stan a chance to try every language he knows.

The Literary and Crafts Center

It's only 25 miles from Waynesville to Asheville. Asheville is crammed with arts, crafts, antiques, literary and music people, and a healthy assortment of free spirits deeply involved in the unique Appalachian culture. The best place for variety and quality to see and buy area crafts is the **Folk Art Center,** just east of town at milepost 382 on the Blue Ridge Parkway, about ¹/₂ mile north of Highway 70. It has been operated by the Southern Highland Handicraft Guild since 1980 and houses permanent and traveling exhibits and the Allanstand Craft Shop, where you can buy items similar to those in the exhibits. Crafts represented include weaving, pottery, basketry, quilting, jewelry, wood carving, stitchery, and musical instruments. Admission free; donations welcomed. Open every day except Thanksgiving, Christmas, and New Year's Day, 9:00 A.M. to 5:00 P.M. Closed occasionally for inventory and changing exhibitions (704-298-7928).

At the edge of town, two well-known attractions here have become almost obligatory stops for anyone who wants to claim to have seen the area: Grove Park Inn and Biltmore Estate. Both nearly defy description. As newspaper writer Jean Thwaite once said of **Grove Park Inn,** "It would almost be ugly, were it not so interesting." The building, of a size that seems to dwarf pyramids, is built of red boulders hauled from Sunset Mountain, on which it's located, in 1913. William Grove did well, to understate matters, in pharmaceuticals in St. Louis. He liked Asheville, so he bought a lot of it, including Sunset Mountain. Then eschewing architects, who didn't understand him, he got his son-in-law to design and build (without a contractor) the massive hotel. The inn is 500 feet long, with a flagstone-floored lobby 80 feet wide and almost half the length of a football field. The fireplaces at each end are so big they burn 12-foot logs, and when there's no fire, children can walk into them upright to play.

George Washington didn't sleep here, but practically everyone else important has: Thomas Edison, Henry Ford, Enrico Caruso, the Roosevelts, Dwight Eisenhower, even F. Scott Fitzgerald. Today the inn is popular with people looking for a place to celebrate a special occasion and with companies and organizations who want somewhere extra nice to gather their members.

After recent additions, the inn has more than 500 rooms. Facilities include five restaurants, four cocktail lounges, indoor and outdoor swimming pools, golf, tennis, racquetball, a fitness center with aerobics room, weight room, Nautilus equipment, whirlpools, and saunas. The accommodations are luxurious; rates are correspondingly high, although they drop considerably in the off-season, when a variety of special packages are available (704–252–2711).

Many of the packages include a tour of the **Biltmore Estate,** which seems appropriate because it operates on the same grand scale. Like Mr. Grove, George Vanderbilt liked Asheville, and he too had a little money. He bought a lot of Asheville too, about 125,000 acres, and had a 250-room private home built on the property. (Today only 7,500 acres belong to the estate. The rest is part of the Blue Ridge Parkway or Mount Pisgah National Forest.) The home was famous from the beginning for its beauty of design and workmanship. The master builders were brought from Europe. The home was also famous for being ahead of its time in its modern conveniences, having early forerunners of washing machines and driers. Art in the mansion includes originals by Bodini, Ming dynasty china, and antiques that belonged to Napoleon.

It will take you the better part of a day to see the place properly, especially if you go beyond the mansion to explore the gardens and visit the winery. Although the Biltmore Estate Winery is still relatively young, some oenophiles say the wines—red, white, rosé, and champagne—are developing nicely. They are for sale, priced in the moderate range. Admission fees to the Biltmore Estate are high. The estate is open daily from 9:00 A.M. to 5:00 P.M. (704-255-1776).

Biltmore Estate and Gardens

If you're not overwhelmed by the grandeur of Biltmore Estate, you're a rare bird. A nice way to decompress and get things back in perspective again is to spend a night at **Cedar Crest,** 674 Biltmore Avenue (704-252-1389). This bed and breakfast inn has ten rooms in the main house and a guest cottage. There are a two-bedroom suite with a parlor and fireplace and a single-bedroom suite with a parlor. This is an 1890 Queen Anne-style Victorian mansion in which the work was purportedly done by the same craftsmen who worked on the Biltmore mansion. Apparently, once they were in this country and established in the little village built for them to work on Biltmore, they decided to hang around afterward and pick up a few odd jobs. Like the Biltmore Estate, Cedar Crest is so full of wonderful features that you can't take them all in at once, but the scale is more human and easier to relate to. The elaborate, first-generation oak woodwork differs in every room, with such subtle distinctions as being heavy and masculine in the library, but delicate and ornate in the dining room, which was considered a ladies' territory. Other special features in the house include a corner fireplace with fluted columns, a gilded cherub, and splendid stained-glass windows. There's a secret closet where silverware used to be hidden in troubled times. And the house has what may be the longest (6 feet) and smallest (4 feet) bathtubs in North Carolina. Jack McEwan will guide you through the splendors of the place with infectious enthusiasm. Then, to hone in on the down-to-earth, creature-comfort level, you need to know about Barbara McEwan's "Victorian hanging garden," as she calls it. At Cedar Crest the bed sheets, after they are washed, are hung out on the clothesline to dry in the sun. If you've never slept inhaling the fragrance of line-dried sheets, you'll have to trust the word of those who have. It's the ultimate sensual delight.

An integral part of Asheville's intellectual and musical activity is Malaprops Bookstore/Cafe, 61 Haywood Street, where the ambience resembles what one imagines for Paris of the 1950s. Emoke Bracz, the owner, writes poetry. Other staff members produce fiction, nonfiction, and cartoons. North Carolina writers, of whom there are an astonishing number, stop in to browse or autograph, depending on their current state of productivity. In the background, music progresses through selections of jazz, New Age, and folk, all of which you can buy in the downstairs cafe, where people sit around sipping coffee concoctions, nibbling desserts, and, presumably, talking either about their own writing or about the books upstairs. The offerings include many titles in poetry, feminist and women's books, American Indian, travel, and North Carolina selections.

The unusual book stock and the unique atmosphere here made Malaprops something of a tourist attraction as well as a local center of the literatti. Interestingly, the store is admired by many other bookstore proprietors and staff in the state. And although Malaprops likes paying customers as much as the next store, old school desks scattered about the place make for comfortable browsing, too (704-254-6734). Open Monday through Saturday, 9:00 A.M. to 8:00 P.M.; in July only, also open Sunday, noon to 5:00 P.M.

While you're feeling literary, visit the **Thomas Wolfe Memo-**

rial, 48 Spring Street. This is the novelist's boyhood home, described in his novel, *Look Homeward Angel,* as "Dixieland." In real life it was called "The Old Kentucky Home." Wolfe's mother, Julia, ran a boardinghouse in the rambling Victorian house, and its various rooms and furnishings, along with local people, were all incorporated into Wolfe's novel, mostly in unflattering terms. The people of Asheville didn't like that one bit, which led to Wolfe's second novel, *You Can't Go Home Again.* After Wolfe died, the townspeople relented, as they often do when a troublesome celebrity stops being troublesome and remains merely famous, and bought the house to turn into a memorial for him. It is now a North Carolina State Historic Site. Visiting the house, which has been kept the same as it was when the Wolfes lived in it and has descriptions from Wolfe's writing in appropriate places so you can compare the words with the reality, goes a long way toward explaining the often gloomy tone of his writing. Nominal admission fee. Open Monday through Saturday, 9:00 A.M. to 5:00 P.M., and Sunday, 1:00 to 5:00 P.M. Shorter hours and closed Mondays November through March. Closed state holidays (704–253–8304).

Just about 10 miles outside Asheville, near Weaverville on Reems Creek Road off Highway 25 north, is another state historic site, the **Zebulon B. Vance Birthplace.** Vance was a Civil War officer, a United States senator, and governor of North Carolina. In fascinating contrast to the splendor of Biltmore Estate, this restored pioneer farmstead has only a five-room log house and some outbuildings. The log house was reconstructed around the original chimneys. The outbuildings, including loom house, spring house, toolshed, smokehouse, corn crib, and slave cabin, are furnished as they would have been between 1795 and 1840. Displays instruct you further in life of the times. Admission free. Open April through October, Monday through Saturday, 9:00 A.M. to 5:00 P.M. and Sunday, 1:00 to 5:00 P.M. November through March, closed Mondays and open shorter hours other days (704–645–6706).

Asheville makes a good center from which to go in four different directions. Following the parkway takes you to New River State Park. A drive of about 20 miles down Interstate 26 takes you into the southern mountains, where Flat Rock, Hendersonville, and Saluda offer many rural pleasures and some interesting crafts and antiques shops. Driving northeast from Asheville along the Blue Ridge Parkway takes you higher into the mountains to Blowing Rock and environs. And a scenic ride east along Interstate 40 and Highway 226 to Polkville brings you back into the lower elevations of the Piedmont.

If you follow the parkway almost to the Virginia border, getting off to drive north on Highway 221, you come to the oldest river in North America and the second oldest (the Nile is older) in the world. It's the only major river in the country that runs south to north. Paradoxically called New River, it meanders peacefully through more than 100 miles of northwestern North Carolina. The name was the result of surveryors' surprise when they finally chanced upon the river they hadn't known about in this remote part of the state in 1749.

You enjoy good access to the river from New River State Park (919-982-2587), an area of breathtakingly lovely mountains, valleys, woods, and fields, 8 miles southeast of Jefferson off Highway 88 on State Road 1588. Compared to other state parks, New River shows up infrequently in travel books and articles, probably because it is in a remote part of the state and because the facilities are primitive. This is the river to find if you like placid canoeing rather than wild races through white water and want fishing spots not bothered by heavy powerboat traffic. There are canoe landings and campgrounds. The woods are great for hiking and are full of spots that cry out for a simple picnic.

Behind the peaceful scene lies the story of a dramatic struggle that isn't anywhere near being over. It started in the 1960s, when Appalachian Power Company planned to build a dam there, raising tremendous public objection. In protective response Congress designated the area a National Wild and Scenic River in 1976, effectively stopping the power company.

But little funding was ever forthcoming to actually buy and protect the land, and gradually a new force is changing the scene along the river: subdivision and development. New houses, roads, and lots are beginning to appear on what was farmland or woodland. There's even a golf course in the works. Although none of it is in the state park, of course, people who like their countryside bucolic and unspoiled are getting nervous, while those who value economic development for the area are digging in their heels and sending out the bulldozers.

Given the usual inclination of those who can afford to build in the prettiest places—high on mountain summits, on beaches and islands, and along rivers—it's hard to say what will happen along the New River in the coming decade. The good news is that the state park is, as locals like to call the river, "a national treasure" and should remain a special place to visit for a long time to come.

On the drive down Interstate 26, one of the most interesting stops is the **Carl Sandburg Home National Historic Site,** a 240-acre farm called Connemara, a bit south of Hendersonville in Flat Rock. Sandburg spent the last twenty-two years of his life here, mostly writing, while his wife and daughter managed the place as a goat farm. his collection of poems, *Honey and Salt,* was written here when he was eighty-five. The poems contrast with such earlier works as "Chicago," reflecting not only the work of an older man, but also of one living in different surroundings. For instance, in the poem "Cahokia," Sandburg writes about an Indian watching a butterfly rise from a cocoon, flowers sprouting in spring, and the sun moving. The Indian, Sandburg writes, doesn't worship the sun, but dances and sings to the "makers and movers of the sun." It takes on added significance when you know that Flat Rock was named for a large granite plateau that had once been a Cherokee sacred ground. Sandburg's life here was influenced not only by the early cycles of nature, but also by Cherokee Indian lore. Similarly, looking across the mountains, it's easy to understand how Sandburg might have arrived at his poem "Shadows Fall Blue on the Mountains."

When you visit Sandburg's study at Connemara, both the man and his poetry seem alive. The study is said to be exactly as he left it, with a shawl tossed over the back of his desk chair, a clunky manual typewriter standing on an upended crate, and stacks of paper and disorderly piles of books everywhere. You may also walk along trails on the grounds where you see the kinds of plants and wildlife from which Sandburg must have drawn many of his images. Nominal admission charged. Open daily except Christmas from 9:00 A.M. to 5:00 P.M. Inquire about some special seasonal activities (704-693-4178).

A pleasant way to sustain the mood of the Sandburg farm a little longer is by staying overnight, or at least for lunch or dinner, at The Woodfield Inn, just 3 blocks away (704-639-6016). This building has been an inn for all of its 135-plus years, and it reflects both the culture and the history of the area. A lot of the furniture has been in the inn since it opened. The original brass hardware is intact. The wallpaper in the entry is an exact reproduction of the original wallpaper. The inn has a secret room where Confederates hid valuables from Yankee troops. Hogarth prints on the walls entertain with their wicked, unsubtle humor. And an abundance of great swordleaf ferns complement the Victorian atmosphere of the dining room. Outside, nature trails winding across twenty-five beautiful acres invite walking and reflecting. Not that you should live by reflection alone. The Woodfield Inn's food, an amalgamation of mountain and continental cuisine emphasizing fresh vegetables, fish, and poultry, as well as southern fried chicken and prime rib, attracts local diners from miles around (704-693-6016).

From Flat Rock you can take a jog over onto Highway 176, driving about 12 miles to Saluda, a little town of less than a thousand people, with a notable concentration of antiques and artisans. Walking around in the little town itself, you find several shops selling local crafts and antiques and a general store run by a pair of women reminiscent of the sisters on "The Waltons'" television show, except, of course, they aren't offering Mason jars full of the "recipe"—as far as anyone knows.

Saluda has two overnight possibilities, quite different from one another. At the top of a steep hill, overlooking Saluda's main street, Dottie Eargle's Woods House has six rooms, including one in a separate cottage. The place is furnished throughout with late Victorian and turn-of-the-century antiques, highlighted by an outstanding collection of old needlework displayed throughout the inn. Dorothy has run an antiques shop for many years, and she has the ability to put together a room as only those intimate with antiques and their earlier uses can. (She cooks breakfast in a real country kitchen that has a wood-burning stove.) The inn (704-749-9562) is open April through October. In the center of town, Dorothy has a real estate office, now grown to three rooms, entirely furnished with antique oak office furniture. If you admire those old, functional oak file cabinets, bookcases, and desks and chairs, it's worth a trip to Saluda just to see the office.

A few miles into the country, in a totally different mood, The Orchard Inn, owned and operated by Ann and Ken Hough, offers you seclusion, a feeling of romance, and gourmet meals. The inn is on eighteen wooded acres at the top of the Saluda rise, 2,500 feet above sea level. Ann has decorated with artistic flair, using plants, crafts, antiques, and wonderful paintings by Ken, in an upscale country style. Ken used to be an opera singer. Probably he was a good one. Today he's a chef, and the evidence of how good he is at it comes to the table every lunch and dinner time: boned duck in mustard sauce, rack of lamb, onion tarts, chicken with raspberry sauce. But he's not one of those slave-all-day-over-a-hot-stove guys. Somehow, Ken manages to be in the parlor chatting with guests or cutting out their profiles with scissors and black paper beside the fireplace, while dinner simmers on to perfection in the kitchen. During busy times the inn has a two-night minimum stay. It is open year-round (704-749-5471). When you call these Saluda telephone numbers, be patient. Sometimes the little local phone company has problems; always through the ringing you hear burbles and rasps like something out of the days of hand-cranked phones, and you feel that a very young Aunt Bea should answer.

The High Country

The next drive you might make from Asheville continues north on the Blue Ridge Parkway to **Mount Mitchell State Park,** elevation 6,684 feet, the highest point in the eastern United States. You'll leave the parkway at milepost 355.4 to take Highway 128 to the fifteen hundred-acre wilderness park. It's a 5-mile drive to the peak, but it will feel a lot longer. The park has hiking trails, picnic areas, a visitor center with maps, camping areas, and a lookout tower from which you can see what must be the most stunning mountain views east of the Mississippi. There are also a restaurant and a refreshment stand. Be careful while you're here. Mount Mitchell is named for Dr. Elisha Mitchell, who fell off the summit and died. Your falling off too probably wouldn't lead to getting the mountain renamed in your honor. The park is closed in winter (704-675-4611).

The next stop you might try along the parkway is at milepost 331, where Highway 226 and State Road 1100 take you to Emerald Village near Little Switzerland. At Emerald Village, established on the site of the Old McKinney and Bon Ami mines, you can visit the North Carolina Mining Museum, which displays the tools used at the height of gem mining in the area. Outdoor displays and a printed trail guide explain the entire mining process, and you have the opportunity to look for your own emeralds, rubies, aquamarines, and the like. More vigorous all-day tours through mines not previously open to the public, complete with hard hats, rock hammers, and a chuck-wagon lunch, are available at scheduled times. If your gem hunting doesn't go well, you can pick up something at the Ore Car Rock Shop or have a rough gem cut, polished, and set into a piece of jewelry at the Cab & Facet Shop. Open 9:00 A.M. to 5:00 P.M., May 1 through October 31. Open an hour longer in the evening from Memorial Day to Labor Day (704-765-6463 or 704-765-4367).

From here you could return to the parkway or go north on Highway 221 to get to **Linville Caverns** and Linville Falls just beyond the caverns. If you're back on the parkway, exit at milepost 317.4 and turn left on Highway 221. Linville Caverns lie under Humpback Mountain and were believed to be forgotten by the white race until about a hundred years ago, when fish that seemed to be swimming out of the mountains caught the attention of explorers. During the Civil War, deserters from troops on both sides hid in the caverns. Today the caverns are lit electrically, showing stalactites and stalagmites and trout that, having always swum in the dark, can't see. Guides lead the tours 2,000 feet underground, pointing out important features and answering questions. Modest admission fee charged. Open June 1 through Labor Day, 9:00 A.M. to 6:00 P.M. Closed at 5:00 P.M. in April, May, September, and October and 4:30 P.M. in March and November. Open weekends only December, January, and February; closed Thanksgiving and Christmas (704-756-4171).

Linville Falls comprises two waterfalls at Linville Gorge, a primeval canyon in the sizable wilderness area given to the Blue Ridge Parkway by John D. Rockefeller. The gorge is the deepest cut east of the Grand Canyon. There are hiking trails and picnic spots.

Still moving north along the parkway, you come to **Grand-father Mountain,** where, if you've got the nerve for it, you can walk across the Mile-High Swinging Bridge, a 218-foot suspension bridge between two peaks that sways in the wind. Should you quite sensibly prefer to put your feet on something more solid, Grandfather Mountain has lots of hiking trails. You'll need to pick up a moderately priced permit and a trail map at the entrance. This is the area where the Scottish Highland Games, open to the public, are held the second weekend in July every year. It is also a spot that attracts hang gliders. Open 8:00 A.M. to dusk summers; closed at 4:30 P.M., sometimes earlier, in winter. Moderate admission fee charged (704-733-4337).

A few minutes farther on Highway 221 brings you to the **Blowing Rock,** a cliff 4,090 feet above sea level that overhangs

Johns River Gorge, 3,000 feet below, at the town of Blowing Rock. Because of the way the gorge is shaped and overhung, air blows upward, making snow appear to fall upside down and throwing upward light objects tossed over the edge. According to the legend of Blowing Rock, a Cherokee brave leaped to his death here to keep his tribe from making him return to the plains, leaving his Chicasaw wife behind. She prayed to the Great Spirit until the sky turned red and the wind blew her brave back up onto the rock. A wind has blown up from the valley ever since. Moderate admission charge. Open April through October, 9:00 A.M. to 6:00 P.M. (704-295-7111).

By the time you get to Blowing Rock, the children will probably have heard of **Tweetsie Railroad,** a family theme park that has been operating in North Carolina since 1956. It's touristy, but kind of fun. Coal-fired steam engines pull the train of open cars through 3 miles of staged events: a train robbery, an Indian raid, and so on. Also, a chairlift carries you up to Mouse Mountain, where you can pan for gold and walk through the petting farm. Another section of the park duplicates a country fair of the early 1900s, right down to the cotton candy. Among other features are an ice cream parlor, a jail, and a firehouse. Moderately high

Tweetsie Railroad

admission charged. Open daily from Memorial Day through October, 9:00 A.M. to 6:00 P.M., with shorter hours and some features closed weekdays after Labor Day (704-264-9061).

Blowing Rock has several places to spend the night, including the long-popular Green Park Inn (704-295-3141) and the newer Meadowbrook Inn (704-295-9341). You are also just 8 miles south of Boone, a commercial resort area where you'll find lots of motels, which, though out of spirit with the off-the-beaten-path traveler, are easy and comfortable when you're tired and just need to sleep.

When you have more energy than that, save it to drive on up into Valle Crucis, close to Boone but totally unlike it in nature. Although the little town sees hundreds and hundreds of visitors, it manages to continue operating and looking like a small town. Its history dates back to 1780, when Samuel Hix, the first known white settler in Valle Crucis, staked a claim to a thousand acres. Later he traded the land for a gun, a dog, and a sheepskin. Eventually it became an Episcopal mission, named *Valle Crucis* because three creeks came together in the shape of a cross. Today the missions serve as a retreat for many church denominations.

People stop most often at the **Mast Store,** an authentic general store listed on the National Register of Historic Places, which still sells penny candy, seeds, leather boots, Woolrich sweaters, flannel shirts, long johns, and just about everything else you can think of, mostly stacked, not too neatly, along wooden shelves. The store has begun sending out a mail-order catalog reminiscent of early L.L. Bean.

The **Mast Farm Inn,** not associated with the store, is just outside the village on State Road 1112 (704-963-5857). Francis and Sibyl Pressly cater to overnight guests and to folks who make reservations for dinner. Mast Farm is also on the National Register of Historic Places, as a restored, self-contained mountain homestead, comprising a spring house, ice house, wash house, barn, blacksmith shop, gazebo, and cabin in addition to the inn. Sleeping here is quiet and comfortable. The antiques are sparingly arranged to avoid a sense of clutter. Eating here is an experience in socializing as well as in tasting. Before dinner, Francis learns a little something about each of the guests and, as he seats them at the long dining room tables, introduces everyone. People chat back and forth throughout the meal, passing platters and talking about their backgrounds and travels. The food goes way beyond standard southern cooking. Each dinner includes, along with the meat and vegetables, a meatless entree. When they serve a roasted pork loin, the meat is separated from the ribs for slicing, and the bones are passed separately for gnawing. Seasonal vegetables come from the farm gardens. Brown bagging is permitted in case you like beer or wine with a good meal.

The Foothills

Instead of heading north from Asheville, you may choose to start east toward the foothills and the Piedmont. Following Interstate 40 east for about 10 miles past Asheville brings you to Black Mountain, an interesting little village that was once a Cherokee Indian center and now is a quiet little pocket for fine-quality mountain crafts. Visiting the **Song of the Wood,** at 203 West State Street, a workshop and sales room devoted to dulcimers and unusual string instruments and their music, leaves you feeling exhilarated and refreshed. Jerry Read Smith makes hammered dulcimers and the even more unusual bowed psaltry, a small triangular instrument played with a violin-type bow, similar to a medieval bowed harp. JoAnn, Jerry's sister, manages the showroom. Everything about the shop is devoted to keeping the old music alive, producing fine-quality handmade instruments, and surrounding you with music.

You're first attracted by the music coming through outside speakers. When you get inside, they'll play lots more music for you. You may hear the music from their independent record albums, "The Strayaway Child," and "Heartdance." The shop sells a highly personal selection of other tapes and albums, mainly hammered dulcimer music, piano music, and Celtic music. The shop is light and airy, with instruments on the walls, a fuel-efficient wood-burning stove, and a mountain rocker. You're invited to sit down and try any of the instruments or listen to the recorded music. If you're interested and ask, you can almost always manage to be shown through the workshop area and have the whole process explained to you. Open from 10:00 A.M. to 5:00 P.M., Monday through Saturday (704-669-7675).

Immediately after Black Mountain, you come to Old Fort, an area that was still considered Cherokee Indian land for some time after white pioneers began pushing in during the middle 1770s. At the beginning of the American Revolution, General Griffith

Rutherford assembled 2,500 troops to attack the Cherokees, who seemed to be siding with the British. Afterward, the Indians conceded a huge portion of land, a pattern that was repeated often up to the time of the Trail of Tears in 1838. In subsequent years, the Western North Carolina Railroad became important here. The Mountain Gateway Museum tells the story, as do the Stepp and Morgan cabins that were moved here later. The site is a branch of the North Carolina Museum of History. It's not a big, splashy place and deserves your attention for that very reason. Admission free. Open daily, 9:00 A.M. to 5:00 P.M., and Sunday, 2:00 to 5:00 P.M. (704-668-9259).

An outdoor treat in the same area is the Catawba Falls Trail, a special place that Eleanor Brawler wrote about for the *Charlotte Observer.* The main falls are the headwaters of the Catawba River. You'll find Catawba River Road at the Old Fort exit off Interstate 40. Follow the road through 3 miles of farmland, where you'll come to a small bridge and a private road at a tree farm. Cross the street to the right bank; walk past an old dam about a mile on, and when the path ends, cross the stream again, to the left bank. Here you should be able to hear the falls, and you'll come to a trail and then a clearing, where you'll find the waterfalls, falling from 200 feet above you. If you're hesitant about hiking into unfamiliar territory, ask in town for advice. Local people know the area.

Brawley suggests a second, shorter hike in the Falls Branch area, to see falls so little known they aren't even named. At Marion, go north from Interstate 40 on Highway 221/226, crossing the Catawba River and passing the River Breeze Restaurant. Drive 5½ miles after crossing the river. Turn left at the Woodlawn Motel and continue on 0.8 miles. The paved road ends. Bear left at the fork on a dirt road far enough to park. At the little bridge, you'll find a trail to the right that wanders through the rhododendrons beside a mountain stream. At the next fork, bear left again to see the falls. The area is also rich in wildflowers.

After these adventures, return to Interstate 40 and drive on to where Highway 226 intersects Interstate 40 at Glenwood. From here, you can enjoy a beautifully scenic drive to Polkville while you also enjoy a good brisk sit. If you're in need of a total collapse by then, try **Patterson's Carriage Shop Bed and Breakfast,** in a beautiful farmhouse that the Pattersons estimate to be somewhere between 110 and 120 years old. It has a big porch on two sides. Only four rooms are available to guests, so staying here is very much like visiting family. The name "Carriage Shop" isn't just for effect; they really do sell all types of two- and four-wheel horse-drawn vehicles. Pat and Nancy are deeply involved with horses. He used to race, and she has Morgan show horses. There are three Arabians on the property. But you're probably more concerned with what Nancy will feed you for breakfast than what she feeds her horses. Breakfast is sufficient, however, to choke a horse, as the old saying puts it: sausage, bacon, eggs, home fries, biscuits, pancakes, French toast. You won't have all these at one breakfast, of course, but you won't go away hungry. Real maple syrup (Nancy calls it "Yankee maple syrup") makes pancakes or French toast a special treat. If you cultivate a taste for it while you are here, you can buy some in the shop, where you'll also find wall hangings and handmade quilts for sale (704-538-3929).

From Polkville, you might want to take a quick drive north on Highway 10 into the little village of **Casar**—pronounced KAYser, population about 340. It's a place you'd never know about unless someone told you. Elizabeth Sturgeon, a woman well under fifty who was raised here, remembers every quaint detail. the people who founded the town meant to call it "Caesar," but somehow they got the spelling wrong, and it's been Casar every since. Until recently, all the major roads were dirt; even today they are not all paved. Where the roads came into the center of this little spot, a stop sign stood—most of the time. Every Saturday night one old gentleman who didn't navigate too well when he was in his cups (homemade 'shine—it was a dry area) ran into it and knocked it down. Every Monday morning, someone put it up again.

Even into our high-tech age, Casar has been a place where electricity, telephones, and indoor plumbing were frills, luxuries nobody wanted. hamburgers and hot dogs were unknown. Today, Elizabeth estimates, 95 percent of the people have power and plumbing. You still could have trouble over the hamburgers and hot dogs with the older folks.

In the center of town you can see what used to be Tom Hoyle's grocery store, where he accepted eggs and chickens in payment for flour and other merchandise.

The school used to serve grades one through twelve and have a phenomenal basketball team. School started early in the season and closed for six weeks during cotton-picking time because all the children, generally ten to twelve to a family, were needed to work in the fields you see around the school. Elizabeth still has her cotton-picking sack. If you look behind the school, you can find the place on the bank where the kids ran down to the store to buy penny suckers with coconut in them.

Elizabeth doesn't live in Casar any more, but she goes back often and finds it only a little changed—more modern in its technology, but the same warm little place as far as its people go. Park your car and walk around awhile. Elizabeth says, "You might get looked at, but somebody will come to see if you need help."

Somehow, Art Linkletter found out about this area and started a golf resort called Pine Mountain Lake about 7 miles on toward Morgantown. Certainly you could get a hamburger in the restaurant there, but the resort hasn't tainted Casar one bit.

When you return to Polkville, pick up Highway 182 to Lincolnton and then Highway 150 on to Mooresville, a town of about nine thousand people, where you can find the necessities of traveling in a congenial environment. Shortly after you pass through Mooresville, still on Highway 150, you'll come to **Carrigan Farms,** a place worth visiting any time of year. By the road in front of rows of greenhouses in a large shelter, you can buy asparagus and hanging baskets in April, strawberries in May and June, fresh vegetables all summer, cider and pumpkins in October, and poinsettias in November and December. Growing produce and plants, with twenty-five people employed, this farm is an effort of Doug and Susan Carrigan, his parents, and his grandparents. Yet this is more than a family farm; it's a farm involved in the community in ways that make you feel good, even though you live somewhere else. For instance, the walls are covered with letters and drawings from school kids who've visited the farm.

Dear Susan and Doug,

Susan, we liked the hayride.

We also liked the way the cow thought your finger was a bottle.

Doug, we liked the way you showed us the honey bees.

We had fun.

Love,
Matthew
Adam
Karen
Michael

Hang around to talk with the people, breathe the clear country air, and pick up whatever is in season. If you call ahead at the right time of year, you can probably even arrange a hayride (704-664-1450).

Acknowledgments

Many of the photographs from which the drawings in this book were made were provided by the North Carolina Division of Travel and Tourism.

Thanks to Mickey Smith and Terry Almond at the Richfield Post Office for providing information about Portsmouth Island. Thanks to John and Elizabeth Sturgeon for telling me about Casar, a town no tourist is likely to find normally. Thanks to the Williamsons at Ocean Isle for arranging a place off the beaten path for me to stay year after year. Thanks to Ron and Adrienne Schrank for helping me learn about Greensboro. Thanks to the people at Jay Howard's studio in Charlotte for keeping me abreast of changes in that city. And, most of all, thanks to the scores of kind North Carolinians who gave me directions, marked my maps, and on occasion actually led me to the proper road all the considerable number of times I got lost.

About the Author

Sara Pitzer, author of *Pennsylvania: Off the Beaten Path* and *Recommended Country Inns South*, has also written several cookbooks and how-to books. She lives on eight acres of woods in a small farming community in North Carolina with two dogs, six cats and one husband—the same husband she's had since 1960 (there's been some turnover in cats and dogs). Her passions, in addition to seeing new places and meeting new people, are cooking and gardening.

Index

Index

D

Darrell's Bar-BQ, **81**
Dilworth Brewing Company, 92
Discovery Place, 91
Dismal Swamp Canal, 39
Dr. Josephus Hall House, 77
Dover Pottery, 58
Duke Homestead State Historic Site and Tobacco Museum, 50
Duke University, 50
Duplin Wine Cellars, 14
Durham, 50

E

Eastway Deli and Cafe, 75
Edenton, 40
1852 Zebulon Latimer House, 9
1868 Stewart-Marsh House, 79
Ella's Restaurant, 3
Elizabethan Gardens, 34
Elizabeth City, 39
Elizabeth II State Historic Site, 34
Eliza's Oyster Bar, 10
Emerald Island, 17
Emerald Village, 109

F

Farm House Gardens, 74
Fearrington Inn, 53
Federal Alley, 26
Fireman's Museum, 27
Fisherman's Wharf Restaurant, 36
Flat Rock, 105
Folk Art Center, 101
Fort Fisher Ferry, 14
Fort Fisher National Historic Site, 13
Fort Raleigh National Historic Site, 33
furniture manufacturing, x, 67

Index

J

K

L

M

Index

Ocracoke, 31
Old Fort, 113
Old Salem, 64
Old Town Beaufort Restoration Tour, 21
Orange County Historical Museum, 52
Orchard Inn, 108
Ore Car Rock Shop, 110
Oriental, 24
Orton Gardens, 9
Oscar's House, 31

P

Palmer-Marsh House, 30
Patterson's Carriage Shop Bed and Breakfast, 114
Perquimans River, 39
Pewter Rose, 92
Pfeiffer College, 83
Phil Morgan Pottery, 57
Piper, Lee, 79
Pittsboro, 52
Polkville, 105
Poplar Grove Plantation, 15
Portsmouth Island, 23
pottery, history of in North Carolina, 55–57
Premier, The, 70
Pringle Pottery, 53

Q

Qualla Arts and Crafts Mutual, Inc., 99
Qualla Boundary Cherokee Indian Reservation, 98

R

Raleigh, 46–48
Raleigh Farmers Market, 48
Randolph House, 96

Index